# SIX SECRET TEACHINGS

A MILITARY CLASSIC FROM ANCIENT CHINA

Cherry Stone Publishing, an imprint of
Sweet Cherry Publishing Limited
Unit 36, Vulcan House,
Vulcan Road,
Leicester, LE5 3EF
United Kingdom

First published by Cherry Stone Publishing in 2021
2021 edition

2 4 6 8 10 9 7 5 3 1

ISBN: 978-1-78226-962-5



*Six Secret Teachings*



Cover design and illustrations
by Sophie Jones

www.cherrystonepublishing.com

Printed and bound in India
I.TP002

# TAIGONG'S

# SIX SECRET TEACHINGS

## ANCIENT CHINESE MILITARY THOUGHTS

CHERRY STONE
PUBLISHING

CHAPTER I.

# CIVIL SECRET TEACHINGS

# KING WEN'S TEACHER

1

King Wen of Zhou was about to go hunting, so his chief history scribe performed divination and told him: "You will get a great catch when you go hunting on the north bank of the Wei River. What you will get is not a dragon, a horse, a tiger or a bear, but a duke or marquis. He is a teacher sent to you by heaven to assist you in your career, and his teachings will benefit the three generations of the imperial family."

2

King Wen asked: "Does the divination really signify this?"

3

The scribe replied: "My ancestor Chou performed divination for Yu the Great and Yu found Gao Yao as a result. The signs back then were similar to those of today."

4

King Wen fasted for three days, then took a hunting cart and drove a hunting horse to the northern bank of the Wei River.

5

He eventually saw Taigong sitting on a grass mat fishing.

6

King Wen went up to him and asked: "Do you enjoy fishing?"

7

Taigong replied: "I have heard that a gentleman enjoys realising his ambition and an ordinary man enjoys doing his own thing. Now my fishing is very much like this. My interest does not lie in fishing itself."

8

King Wen asked: "What do you mean by saying fishing is very much like this?"

9

Taigong replied: "Fishing is like using people; there are three kinds of authority: to buy talents with a generous salary, to buy soldiers who are willing to die with money; to recruit talents with official positions. These are all like fishing with bait. Fishing is the means to get what you want; its nature is profound with greater principles."

10

King Wen said: "I would like to hear about its profound nature."

11

Taigong replied: "When the source is deep, the water runs endlessly; when the water runs endlessly, fish survive.

12

This is the law of nature. When the roots are deep, the branches and leaves flourish, and fruits will be borne.

13

This is the law of nature. When a gentleman finds like-minded peers, they can work together and build a grand career. This is the law of nature.

14

Words are uttered to adorn the true feelings, and the ability to speak the truth is the best practice.

15

Now I am telling the truth without avoiding any topic, so will you find it unpleasant?”

16

King Wen said: "Only those who have the quality of benevolence and virtue can accept straightforward advice and not be disgusted by the truth. How could I not appreciate it?"

17

Taigong replied: "When the fishing line is thin and the bait is visible, small fish will take the bait; when the line is heavier and the bait is fragrant, medium-sized fish will take the bait; when the line is thick and long and the bait is generous, large fish will take the bait.

18

The fish will be held by the fishing line if they want to eat fragrant bait; men will obey the monarch's appointment if they want to get their salaries.

19

Therefore, if you fish with bait, the fish will be cooked; if you attract talents with titles and salary, the talents will be used to exhaust their ability; if you seize a state with the strength of your family, the state will be taken as your own; if you take the world with the strength of your state, the whole world will be conquered.

20

Alas! The land is vast and the kingdom is thriving, but what they accumulate will eventually go up in smoke.

21

Things are silent and unmoving and secretly prepared, but their light will shine in all directions.

22

How subtle is that! The virtue of a sage ruler lies in the ingenious and subtle management of talents.

23

How joyful is that! The thing that the sage contemplates is to make everyone under heaven have his own way, and to establish all kinds of ways to win the hearts of the people."

24

King Wen inquired: "How do we do to win hearts and minds of all?"

25

Taigong replied: "The world is not one person's world, but a world shared by all people under heaven.

26

He who can share the benefits of the world with all the other will conquer the world, but he who has the benefits of the world only to himself will lose the world.

27

Heaven has its seasons and earth has its wealth.

28

Sharing them with the people is true benevolence.

29

Where benevolence is, the people of the world will give their allegiance.

30

He who saves the people from death, solves their suffering, removes their scourges, and rescues them from distress is a man of virtue.

31

Where virtue is found, the people of the world will give their allegiance.

32

Righteousness is the ability to share with the people's sorrows, happiness, likes and dislikes.

33

Where there is righteousness, the people of the world will strive to follow.

34

People hate death and are happy to live, and welcome benevolence and pursue benefits in accordance with the way.

35

Where the way resides, all under heaven will give their allegiance."

36

King Wen bowed and said: "Words of wisdom! How dare I not accept the will of heaven!" So he invited Taigong onto the hunting cart and returned together to the capital, establishing him as his teacher.

## FULLNESS AND EMPTINESS

1

King Wen asked Taigong: "What is the reason for the chaos and bustle of the world? Some states are strong and some are weak; some are stable and some are chaotic. Is it due to the wise and unwise rulers? Is it the result of the natural transformations of the seasons of heaven?"

2

Taigong replied: "If the ruler is not wise, his state will be in danger and the people will be in chaos; if the ruler is wise, the state will be stable and the people will be obedient.

3

Therefore, the woes and blessings of the Zhou family lie in the fortune and misfortune of the ruler, not in the changes of the mandate of heaven."

4

King Wen inquired: "May I hear about the sages of antiquity?" Taigong replied: "When Emperor Yao ruled, the people called him a sage."

5

King Wen asked: "What was his governance like?"

6

Taigong replied: "During his reign, he did not use gold, silver, pearls and jade as ornaments; he did not wear embroidered and gorgeous clothes; he did not admire precious and exotic objects; he did not cherish antique and precious items; he did not listen to obscene music; he did not decorate the walls of the palace; he did not decoratively carve the beams, square and round rafters and pillars; and he did not even trim the grass in the courtyard.

7

He used deer fur to protect himself from the cold and simple cloth to cover his body; he ate coarse millet and unpolished grains and drank soup made with rough vegetables.

8

He did not delay the farming and weaving of the people through labour service.

9

He restrained his desires and curbed his greed, and ruled the world in a non-action manner.

10

Those officials who were loyal and law-abiding were promoted to higher ranks, and those who were honest and loved the people had their salaries increased.

11

Among the people, those who were filial to the elders and loved the younger ones were given respect, and those who did their best in farming were given encouragement.

12

He distinguished between good and evil and honoured the good people.

**13**

He promoted fairness and integrity, rectified code of conduct and prohibited evil and fraud by law.

**14**

He rewarded those whom he hated for their merits, and punished those whom he loved for their crimes.

**15**

He supported widows and widowers, orphans and solitary elderly people.

**16**

He provided relief to those who suffered from natural or man-made disasters. He led a frugal life, and levied little taxation and labour.

17

Therefore, the people of the world were rich and happy without hunger and cold, and they adored him as if he were the sun and the moon, and were close to him as if he were their parent."

18

King Wen said: "What a great and virtuous sage ruler!"

## AFFAIRS OF STATE

1

King Wen asked Taigong: "I would like to know the fundamental principle of ruling a state. What should be done so that the ruler will be honoured and the people will be at peace?"

2

Taigong replied: "Just love your people."

3

King Wen: "How does one love his people?"

4

Taigong: "Give them profits, do not harm their interests; make them successful, do not hinder their affairs; protect their existence, do not kill them; give them benefits, do not take away; make them happy, do not cause pain; give them pleasure, do not provoke them."

5

King Wen: "Would you please elaborate?"

6

Taigong: "If the people do not lose their occupations, they gain benefits; if farming seasons are not delayed, they make things happen for them; if penalties are reduced, they protect their survival; if fewer taxes are levied, they acquire benefits; if fewer official mansions and pavilions are built, they are happy; if the officials are clean and do not harass and exploit them, they have pleasure.

7

On the contrary, to make the people lose their jobs is to harm their interests; to delay the farming seasons is to corrupt the people's affairs; to punish the people despite their innocence is to kill them; to levy heavy taxes is to plunder the people; to build palaces and pavilions with great construction and fatigue the people is to increase their suffering; to have corruptive officials is to provoke the anger of the people.

8

Therefore, a wise ruler shall govern his people like a parent who loves his children and a brother who loves his younger siblings.

9

He worries about them when he sees them hungry and cold; he grieves for them when he sees them suffering.

10

Reward and punishment shall be implemented as if being imposed upon himself.

11

Taxes shall be levied as if taking from himself.

12

This is the way to love the people."

## THE GREAT FORMS OF ETIQUETTE

1

King Wen asked Taigong: "What are the proper forms of etiquette between a ruler and his ministers?"

2

Taigong replied: "The most important thing for a ruler is to understand the feelings of his ministers, and the most important thing for ministers is to be submissive and respectful.

3

A ruler must not be distant from his ministers, and ministers must not conceal their personal feelings.

4

A ruler must show favour to all, and ministers must fulfil their duties.

5

To show favour is to be all-encompassing like heaven, and to fulfil duties is to be steady and solid like earth.

6

The ruler should follow the example of heaven, and ministers should follow the example of earth, so that the rites and laws between the ruler and his subjects will be fully constituted."

7

King Wen asked: "How should the ruler act?"

8

Taigong replied: "You should be serene and steady but calm and quiet, gentle and temperate but with a clear mind, good at giving favours but not competing with the people for profits, modest and quiet but fair and unselfish, and fair and upright in dealing with affairs."

9

King Wen asked: "How should the ruler listen to advice?"

10

Taigong replied: "Do not accept it rashly, nor reject it rudely.

11

If you accept advice rashly, you will easily lose your opinion, and if you reject it rudely, you will close off the access of speech.

12

A ruler should be like a high mountain, which people look up to, and like an abyss, which people cannot fathom.

13

The virtue of a wise ruler is to be pure and just to the utmost."

14

King Wen asked: "How can the ruler achieve insight into everything?"

15

Taigong replied: "The eyes are valuable in seeing things clearly; the ears are valuable in listening to opinions sensitively; and the mind is valuable in thinking things through.

16

If you rely on the eyes of the world to observe things, you can see everything; if you use the ears of the world to listen to opinions, you can hear everything; if you use the minds of the world to think, you can know everything.

17

When information under all circumstances are gathered just like the spokes converging on the hub of a wheel, the ruler will naturally be able to see everything without being blinded."

## CLEAR INSTRUCTIONS

1

When King Wen was bedridden, he summoned Taigong, and Prince Ji Fa was also at his bedside.

2

King Wen said: "Alas! The heaven is about to end my life.

3

The great affairs of the Zhou state are about to be entrusted to you.

4

Now I would like to hear your words of wisdom, so that they can be clearly passed on to future generations."

5

Taigong replied: "Your Majesty, what do you want to ask about?"

6

King Wen asked: "What are the ways of governance by the ancient sages that should be abandoned and what should be implemented?"

7

Taigong replied: "To be lax in doing good things; to be hesitant in deciding when the time comes; and to be tolerant when one knows one's mistakes – these are the three ways of ruling that should be abolished.

8

To be gentle but quiet; to be humble but respectful; to be strong but claim to be weak; and to be patient but strong – these are the four ways of ruling that should be promoted.

9

Therefore, if justice prevails over selfish desires, the state will prosper; if selfish desires prevail over justice, the state will perish; if respect prevails over slackness, the state will be auspicious; if slackness prevails over respect, the state will perish."

## SIX PRESERVATIONS

1

King Wen asked Taigong: "How does the monarch who rules the state and the people come to lose his position?"

2

Taigong replied: "He is not cautious about the people he employs.

3

The monarch shall have 'six preservations' and 'three treasures'."

4

King Wen asked: "What are 'six preservations'?"

5

Taigong replied: "The first one is benevolence; the second righteousness; the third loyalty; the fourth faith; the fifth courage, and the sixth strategy – these are 'six preservations'."

6

King Wen asked: "How can we carefully select a person who meets the criteria of the 'six preservations'?"

## 7

Taigong replied: "Make him rich to test whether he oversteps the rites and laws; make him honourable to test whether he is arrogant and untamed; entrust him with important tasks to test whether he is steadfast in accomplishing them; order him to deal with problems to test whether he is concealing and deceiving; put him in danger to test whether he is fearless in the face of adversity; let him handle unexpected incidents to to test whether he is able to cope with daunting tasks.

## 8

He who is rich and does not overstep the bounds of propriety is a man of benevolence; he who is honoured but not arrogant is a man of justice; he who is entrusted with an important task and does it with determination is a man of loyalty; he who deals with problems without concealment or deception is a man of faith; he who is in danger but is not afraid is a man of courage; and he who deals with unexpected events with ease is a man of strategy.

9

A monarch should not give the 'three treasures' to others; if he does so, the monarch will lose his authority."

10

King Wen asked: "What are the 'three treasures'?"

11

Taigong replied: "Great agriculture, great labour, and great commerce are referred to as the 'three treasures'.

12

When farmers are organised and gathered in one place to produce, there will be enough food; when craftsmen are organised and gathered in one place to produce, there will be enough implements; when merchants are organised and gathered together to trade, there will be enough wealth and goods.

13

If these three industries are allowed to work in peace, the people will not think of any disturbance.

14

The regional structure should not be confused, and the family organisation of the inhabitants should not be broken up.

15

Make the subjects not richer than the ruler, and the cities not larger than the capital.

16

When the 'six preservations' are fully implemented, the monarch will prosper and develop; when the 'three treasures' are developed and perfected, the state will be secure and stable."

# PRESERVING THE STATE'S TERRITORY

1

King Wen asked Taigong: "How can one preserve the state's territory?"

2

Taigong replied: "Do not alienate the clans; do not neglect the people; be conciliatory to the neighbouring states on the right and left and control the four directions of the world.

3

Do not delegate the power of governing to others; by delegating the power of governing to others, the ruler will lose his authority.

4

Do not dig valleys deeper to increase hills, and do not abandon the foundation to manage the branches.

5

When the sun is bright, seize the opportunity to dry things; when you take up a knife, seize the time to slaughter; when you have an axe, seize the time to conquer.

6

If you don't dry things in the sun at the height of the day, you will lose the timing; if you don't slaughter with a knife, you will lose the profits; if you don't kill the enemy with an axe in your hand, the enemy will take advantage of the situation.

7

If a trickle of water is not blocked, it will become a great river.

8

If a faint spark is not extinguished, it will become a blazing fire and nothing can be done about it; if a sapling is not eliminated, it will eventually have to be cut down with an axe.

9

Therefore, the ruler must strive to make his state rich.

10

Without affluence, you cannot practice benevolent rule; and without benevolent rule, you cannot unite the clansmen.

11

If you alienate your own clansmen, you will suffer, and if you lose your own people, you will fail.

12

Do not loan the power of ruling the state to others, and if you give the ruling power to others, you will be victimised and will not end well."

13

King Wen asked: "What do you mean by benevolence and righteousness?"

14

Taigong replied: "Respect for one's people and unity with one's clansmen.

15

If you respect the people, you will have harmony, and if you unite your clansmen, you will rejoice.

**16**

This is the rule for practising benevolence and righteousness.

**17**

Do not let anyone usurp your authority, but conduct affairs according to your own understanding of common sense.

**18**

To those who are obedient to you, you should be gracious and appoint them; to those who are opposed to you, you should use force to destroy them.

**19**

Follow the above principles without hesitation, and the world will be harmonious and tamed."

# PRESERVING THE STATE

1

King Wen asked Taigong: "How can one preserve the state?"

2

Taigong replied: "Please fast first, and then I will tell you about the laws that run between heaven and earth, the reasons for the growth of all things in all seasons, the truths of the sages in governing state, and the root cause of the transformation of the people's hearts."

3

King Wen then fasted for seven days and asked Taigong again with a bow.

4

Taigong replied: "There are four seasons under heaven, and earth produces all things.

5

There are people under heaven, who are governed by the sages.

6

The law of spring is nourishment and everything is thriving; the law of summer is growth and everything is prosperous; the law of autumn is harvest and everything is full and ripe; the law of winter is storage and everything is hidden and immobile.

7

Everything should be stored away when they are ripe; and after they are stored away, they will grow again.

8

There is neither an end nor a beginning to this cycle. The sages follow this law of nature as a general principle for governing the world.

9

Therefore, when the world is ruled, the sages will remain hidden; when the world is in turmoil, the sages will rise up to set things right and build up their careers.

10

This is the inevitable law. The sages are between heaven and earth, and their position are indeed significant.

11

They follow the common sense to govern the world and make the people stable.

12

The uncertainty of the people's mind is an opportunity for turmoil to occur.

13

When such an opportunity arises, the struggle for power in the world must also arise.

14

At this time, the sages develop their power secretly, and when the time is ripe, they will fight openly.

15

First of all, when they advocate the elimination of violence and peace, the world is bound to respond.

16

When the turmoil has subsided and everything has returned to normal, there is no need to fight for merit, nor to abdicate.

17

In this way, the state will be able to coexist with heaven and earth, and with the sun and the moon."

## HONOURING THE WORTHY

1

King Wen asked Taigong: "As a ruler, what people should be honoured, what people should be suppressed, what people should be appointed, and what people should be removed? What should be strictly forbidden and what should be stopped?"

2

Taigong replied: "As a ruler, you should honour those who are virtuous and talented, suppress those who are not virtuous and talented; appoint those who are loyal and trustworthy, and eliminate those who are deceitful and hypocritical. You should forbid riotous behaviour and stop extravagance. So a ruler should be on guard against the 'six thieves' and the 'seven evils'."

3

King Wen said: "I would like to know about them."

4

Taigong replied: "The 'six thieves' are: first, those among the ministers who build palaces, ponds, and pavilions for pleasure and enjoyment will corrupt the virtue of the ruler.

5

Second, if there are people who do not engage in agriculture and sericulture; who do not rein in their temper; who do whatever they want without scruples; who violate the law; and who do not obey superiors, they will corrupt the monarch's edification.

6

Third, if any of the ministers and officials are in the business of forming cliques and squeezing out the wise and virtuous; and if they obstruct the monarch's clarity, they will undermine the monarch's power.

7

Fourth, those who are arrogant; who boast of their virtue; who are self-important; who make friends with vassals outside; and who do not respect the monarch will undermine the monarch's majesty.

8

Fifth, those who despise their titles and superiors and are ashamed to take risks and who create difficulties for the monarch will undermine the enthusiasm of the meritorious officials.

9

Sixth, the strong clans and big families who compete for plunder and oppress the poor and weak will harm the people's livelihood.

10

The 'seven evils' are: first, they do not have wisdom and power; and in order to obtain a higher official title, they act brave and strong and go to war rashly and take their chances in war; these people should not be appointed as the general and commanders.

11

Second, they have a false reputation but no substance; their words are inconsistent; they conceal the good but promote the evil and take advantage of other people; the ruler must be cautious and must not work with these people.

12

Third, they look simple in appearance and are shabbily dressed; they claim to be doing nothing, but are actually seeking fame; they claim to have no desire, but are actually seeking profit.

13

These are hypocritical people, and the ruler must not be close to them.

14

Fourth, they wear a peculiar hat and gorgeous clothes; they are knowledgeable and eloquent and take pleasure from empty talks; they live in a remote and humble place and specialise in slandering the customs of the time.

15

These are wicked people, and the ruler must not favour them.

16

Fifth, they are slanderous, flattering and unscrupulous in order to get official titles; they are reckless and rash, and greedy about salary.

17

These people should not be appointed by the ruler because they do not care about the major affairs and only speak to please the ruler.

18

Sixth, they engage in extravagant crafts such as carving, engraving and ornamentation, thus harming agricultural production and must be forbidden by the ruler.

19

Seventh, the ruler must stop those who use deceitful tricks, strange techniques, witchcraft, charms and spells to confuse and deceive the good people.

20

Therefore, if the people do not do their best in farming, they are not good people; if the scholars are not faithful and trustworthy, they are not good scholars; if the ministers do not dare to speak straightforwardly and advise, they are not good ministers; if the officials are not fair and honest and love the people, they are not good officials.

21

If the chancellors do not enrich the state and strengthen the army, reconcile all kinds of conflicts, deal with all kinds of problems, ensure that the monarch's position is stable, reorganise the discipline, verify the rites and the truth, and strictly punish and reward, they are not good chancellors.

22

The ruler shall act like the head of a dragon; he is far-sighted and sees everything, observes problems deeply and listens to opinions carefully.

23

He shows solemnity and hides his true feelings. He makes people feel that he is as high as the sky and as deep as the abyss and cannot be fathomed. Therefore, when a ruler is angry but does not show, treacherous ministers will arise; when he should kill but does not, great chaos will follow.

24

If his military power is not exercised, then the enemy states will be empowered."

25

King Wen said: "Excellent!"

# ADVANCING THE WORTHY

1

King Wen asked Taigong: "The ruler is committed to employing wise and capable people. But the state is increasingly chaotic to the point that he is endangered and perishes. Why is that?"

2

Taigong replied: "To select the wise and capable but not to appoint them is to have the false gesture of advancing the worthy, but not the substance of it."

3

King Wen asked: "What is the cause of that?"

4

Taigong replied: "The reason for this is that the ruler tends to appoint people who are popularly praised by the world, and thus he cannot get truly virtuous people."

5

King Wen asked: "Why is that?"

6

Taigong replied: "If a ruler takes those who are praised by the world as virtuous and those who are denigrated by the world as unworthy, then the larger cliques will be appointed and the smaller cliques be rejected. As a result, the wicked will form factions to obscure the wise; the faithful will be put to death for no crime; and the treacherous will cheat their way to titles with their false reputation; the society will become more and more chaotic and the state will not be able to avoid peril."

7

King Wen asked: "How does one advance the worthy?"

8

Taigong replied: "The commanders and ministers shall divide the responsibility to select the virtuous according to the positions and conditions.

9

They shall assess the actual performance of officials according to their duties and examine their abilities, so that their virtues and talents are commensurate with their official positions, and their official positions are in proportion with their virtues and talents.

10

In this way, we have mastered the principles and methods of advancing the worthy."

# REWARD AND PUNISHMENT

1

King Wen asked Taigong: “Reward is used to encourage people and punishment is used to warn people. I want to reward one person to encourage a hundred other people and punish one person to warn the public, what should I do?”

2

Taigong replied: “Reward is to keep faith, and punishment is to do what is necessary. Reward and punishment shall be exercised so that the people can hear and see; even for those who cannot hear and see, the influence of reward and punishment shall be felt. The ruler’s integrity is able to travel smoothly between heaven and earth and up to the gods, not to mention to reach his people!”

## THE WAY OF MILITARY

1

King Wu asked Taigong: "What is the way of military?"

2

Taigong replied: "There is no more important principle for the way of military than a high degree of unity in command. With unity of command, the army can go alone and be invincible.

3

The Yellow Emperor noted that: 'Unity of command conforms to the way of military, so that one can reach the supreme level of managing the army.' The key to applying the principle of unified command is to seize the moment; the key to displaying this principle is to use the trend; the key to mastering this principle is the monarch.

4

That is why the ancient sage kings called war a murderous weapon and used it only as a last resort. Now the king of Shang only knows that his state is existing, but now that it is already in danger; he only knows pleasures, but not the looming disasters.

5

Whether a state can survive or not is not a matter of whether it exists at the moment, but whether it can think of danger in peace; whether a ruler can enjoy himself or not is not a matter of whether he enjoys himself at the moment, but whether he can be happy without forgetting his worries.

6

Now that Your Majesty is reflecting on the fundamental issue of security and survival of your state, why worry about other secondary issues?"

7

King Wu asked: "When two armies meet, the enemy cannot come to attack us, and we cannot go to attack them, either. Both sides have set up strong defences, but neither dares to be the first to attack. What should we do if we want to launch an attack but lack favourable conditions?"

8

Taigong replied: "We should feign chaos on the outside, but actually be strict and tidy on the inside; pretend to lack food on the outside, but actually be well stocked; pretend to be weak, but actually strong in battle.

9

Make the formations either united or separated, gathered or scattered, and pretend to be lacking restraint and discipline to confuse the enemy.

10

Conceal our schemes and keep our intentions secret; raise and consolidate our barriers. Hide our elite troops.

11

Keep our soldiers quiet and invisible so that the enemy have no way to know the deployment of our troops.

12

If you want to launch an attack from the west, you shall first make a feint from the east."

13

King Wu asked: "If the enemy already know the situation of our army and figure out our strategy, what should we do?" Taigong replied: "The way to win is to perceive the enemy's situation thoroughly, seize a favourable opportunity for battle, and deliver a swift and violent blow by surprise."

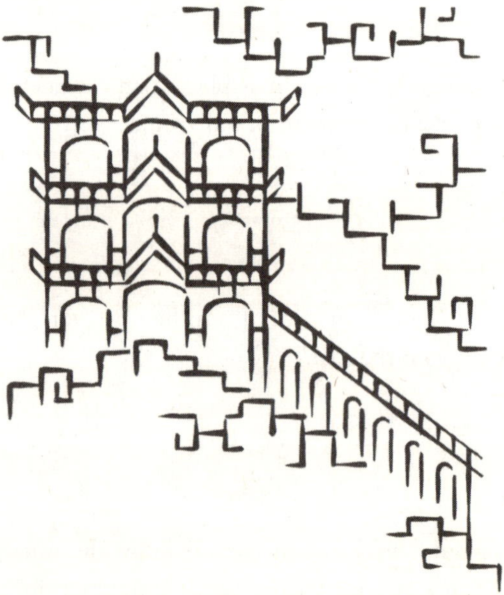

CHAPTER II.

# MARTIAL SECRET TEACHINGS

# OPENING INSTRUCTIONS

1

King Wen of Zhou summoned Taigong in Feng and said to him: "Alas! King Zhou of Shang has become tyrannical to the extreme, killing innocent people at will. I ask you to assist me in saving the people of the world. What do you think should be done?"

2

Taigong replied: "The ruler should cultivate virtue, be courteous to the virtuous, and show favour to the people in order to observe the mandate of heaven.

3

When there are no ominous signs, you should not advocate conquest first; when there are no ill omens, you should not initiate a revolt first.

4

You must see both the natural disaster and the human disaster before you can plan to raise the army to conquer.

5

You must know the tyrant's words and deeds and understand his secret activities to know his true thoughts; you must see his external performance and understand his inner situation to know his true intentions; you must see whom he distances himself from and understand whom he is close to to find out his true emotions.

6

By practising 'the way', your political ideal can be realised; by following the right approach, the purpose of unifying the world can be achieved; by establishing a proper system, success is sure to be achieved; by establishing a strong and dominant position, a powerful enemy can be defeated.

7

Achieving total victory without battle and facing the enemy with a large army without casualties is the use of the army like a god.

8

How remarkable is that! How subtle is that!

9

If you can rescue others who share the same affliction; preserve others who share the same emotions; and help others who share the same hatred and interests, then you will win without armoured soldiers, attack without chariots, and defend without ditches.

10

True wisdom does not reveal wisdom; true strategy does not reveal strategy; true bravery does not reveal bravery; and true interest does not reveal interest.

11

He who works for the good of the world is welcomed by all the people of the world; he who causes all the people of the world to suffer is opposed by all the people of the world.

12

The world is not the world of one man, but the world of all men.

13

To take over the world is like hunting and chasing a wild beast, where everyone has the desire to share the flesh of the beast; it is also like crossing a river in the same boat: if the crossing is successful, everyone achieves the goal and if it fails, everyone suffers.

14

If he does so, all the people of the world will welcome him and will not oppose him.

15

He does not plunder from the people, but is able to get benefits from them; he does not plunder from other states, but is able to get benefits from them; he does not plunder from the world, but is able to get benefits from the world.

16

By not plundering from the people, he is supported by them; and this is the benefit given to him by the people.

17

By not plundering from other states, he is assisted by them; and this is the benefit given to him by the other states.

18

By not plundering from the world, he is embraced by the world; and this is the benefit given to him by the world.

19

Therefore, 'the way' lies in what cannot be seen; affairs lie in what cannot be heard; and victory lies in what cannot be known.

20

How subtle is that! How subtle is that!

21

When an eagle is about to attack, it will first draw in its wings and fly low; when a wild beast is about to fight, it will first lie down with its ears to the ground; when a sage is about to act, he will first show his foolishness and slowness to others.

22

Now in the Shang dynasty, rumours and social turmoil rage, while King Zhou continues his lavish and extravagant lifestyle.

23

This is a sign of the downfall of his reign.

24

I have observed their fields, where weeds overwhelm the seedlings; I have observed their ministers, who are more treacherous than loyal; I have observed their officials, who are tyrannical, cruel, and disobedient.

25

In the face of this situation, their court is still negligent. The time has come for their demise.

26

When the sun rises in the sky, everything under heaven will be bathed in sunlight; when justice is done, everything under heaven will be benefited; when a great army rises, everything under heaven will be glad to join it.

27

Great is the virtue of the sages! Their insight is unique and no one can match it. This is the greatest joy!"

## CIVIL INSTRUCTIONS

1

King Wen asked Taigong: "What principle should a sage follow in governing the world?"

2

Taigong replied: "Without stopping anything or worrying about anything, all things under the heaven will flourish.

3

The decree should be carried out in such a way that the people will be converted without knowing, just as the passage of time.

4

When a sage follows this principle, everything under the sun will be transformed, and the virtuous cycle will be endless.

5

This kind of relaxed and leisurely approach must be repeatedly explored by the ruler.

6

Having sought it, he must not fail to hide it in his heart; having hidden it in his heart, he must not fail to carry it out; having carried it out, he need not tell the world the secret of it.

7

Heaven and earth do not proclaim their laws, but everything grows according to them; sages do not show off their wisdom, but they can achieve glorious achievements.

8

The ancient sages gathered people into families, many families into states, and many states into the world.

9

They assigned wise men as vassals of various states. This is called the rule of the world.

10

They advocated education, conformed to the customs of the people, adapted the customs from time to time, and transformed the evil into righteousness.

11

Although the customs of each state were different, the people were able to live and work in peace and happiness, and everyone respected and loved the ruler.

12

This is called political stability. Alas! In antiquity, the sages were devoted to quietness and inactivity, and the wise rulers are devoted to righteousness of mind and body.

13

The foolish rulers, however, were unable to right his mind and body, so they struggled with the people.

14

When the ruler's decrees were too many, the punishment would be too harsh; and when the punishment was too harsh, the people would be worried; when the people were worried, they would try to escape.

15

Consequently, the upper and lower classes were unsettled and the society descended into turmoil for a long time. This is called political failure.

16

The hearts and minds of the people in the world are like the flow of water. When the way is blocked, it stops. When the way is open, it flows. When it flows quietly, it stays clear. Alas! How remarkable is that! When sages saw the beginning, they knew the end."

17

King Wen asked: "How can I tranquillise the world?"

18

Taigong replied: "Heaven has certain laws of change, and the people have means of livelihood in which they are constantly engaged.

19

If a ruler can appreciate his people's livelihood, the world will be tranquil.

20

Therefore, the best politics is to govern in accordance with the will of the people, and the second best is to preach to convince them.

21

Therefore, the way of heaven can nourish all things without doing anything, and the people can have enough food and clothing without charity. This is the virtuous rule of a sage king.

22

King Wen said: "What you said accords with what I hold dear.

23

I will think bear in mind your teachings all the time and never forget them, making them the fundamental principle of governing the world."

17

Seventh, make the enemy king believe in us by offering generous gifts; at the same time, buy over his close ministers and give them secret benefits.

18

In so doing, both the king and ministers will neglect the development of their state, resulting in a lack of money, food and an empty national treasury.

19

Eighth, bribe the enemy king with valuable treasures, and then take advantage of the opportunity to conspire with him to attack another state and promise benefits.

20

When he gets the benefits, he will trust us, and this will bring the enemy closer to us.

**21**

The closer the relationship, the more the enemy state can be used by us.

**22**

If one rules a state but is externally controlled, he will eventually suffer a terrible defeat.

**23**

Ninth, honour the enemy king with praise and help him solve problem; make him feel that he rules all over the world and bow to his will to win his trust.

**24**

Put him in a supreme position and claim his merits to be even greater than the sages. Then he will certainly be arrogant and neglect administration.

25

Tenth, pretend to be humble and submissive to the enemy king, so as to gain his trust and thus obtain inside information.

26

Obey him and be close to him as if he is a brother. After gaining his trust, we can gradually manipulate him and erode his power in a subtle way. Then when the ultimate time comes, he will think it is the will of heaven to destroy him.

27

Eleventh, block up his access of information. There is no official who does not love riches and loathe death and calamity.

28

Promise them honourable official positions and secretly give treasures to buy over meritorious officials and warriors from the enemy state.

29

Pretend to be poor to the enemy state while stocking up resources internally.

30

Bond with wise and resourceful men from the enemy state to plot with them. Befriend warriors of the enemy state to boost the morale of our army.

31

Satisfy as much as possible the desires of these people to help them gain wealth and prosperity, and to make their appetite for profit insatiable. Then the wise men of the enemy state will deflect. This is called blocking the access of information.

32

How can the enemy king maintain his rule when his access of information is blocked because his officials betray him?

33

Twelfth, confuse the enemy king's mind by endorsing his treacherous ministers; befuddle him by introducing beautiful women and licentious music; wear him down by giving him good dogs and horses, so that the ruler's body is exhausted by indulging in dogs and horses; report good news to him regularly so that he will relax vigilance. Then team up with the other states to seize the right moment to challenge him.

34

After the above twelve methods are correctly applied, military actions can be taken.

35

This is called observing the heavenly omens from above and the geographical positions from below, and when all kinds of favourable signs have been manifested, it is time to raise an army to crush the enemy."

# INSTRUCTIONS ON ACCORDING WITH THE PEOPLE

1

King Wen asked Taigong: "How can one do to govern the world well?"

2

Taigong replied: "If you have more strength than the world, then you can encompass the world; if you have more integrity than the world, then you can restrain the world; if you have more love than the world, then you can be gentle to the world; if you have more grace than the world, then you can keep the world; if you have more authority than the world, then you cannot lose the world; if you are decisive and do not hesitate, you act as firmly as the movement of the celestial bodies and the change of the four seasons. When these six conditions are fulfilled, then the world can be governed.

3

Therefore, he who works for the good of the world is welcomed by all the people of the world; he who causes all the people of the world to suffer is opposed by all the people of the world; he who brings misfortune to the people of the world will be resisted by the people of the world; he who kills the people of the world will be hated by the people of the world; he who conforms to the will of the people of the world will be obeyed by the people of the world; he who causes poverty to the people of the world will be despised by the people of the world; he who makes the people of the world live and work in peace and happiness will be relied upon by the people of the world; he who brings distress to the people of the world will be considered as bane by the people of the world.

4

The world is not one man's world; only a man of morality can assume the position of power."

# THREE DOUBTS

1

King Wu asked Taigong: "I want to build a successful career, but I have three doubts: I am afraid that my strength is not enough to attack the enemy king's strong army; I am afraid that I cannot estrange his cronies; and I am afraid that I cannot disperse his people. What do you think should be done?"

2

Taigong replied: "First, we should take advantage of situations; second, we should use prudent schemes, and third, we should use material resources.

3

When you attack a strong enemy, you must encourage the enemy to be even stronger and more arrogant.

4

What is too strong will certainly break and what is too arrogant will lead to mistakes.

5

To attack a powerful enemy, you must first encourage violence; to divide the enemy's cronies, you must first buy over the enemy's favourite officials; to break up the enemy's army, you must first win the hearts of their people.

6

The most important thing is to be wise in the use of strategies.

7

Promising some benefits to the enemy and giving them advantages will inevitably lead to contention within the enemy.

8

In order to alienate the enemy ruler from his ministers, give his favoured officials benefits according to their preferences and promise them lucrative returns, so that they will be estranged from the ruler and cannot achieve anything.

9

Please them with profits that we offer so that they will not be suspicious of our agenda.

10

The method of attacking a powerful enemy is to first obfuscate the enemy king's clarity, and then to assault his army and destroy his state in order to relieve the suffering of his people.

11

Corrupt him with women; seduce him with lucrative benefits; pamper him with delicacies, and confuse him with lustful pleasures.

12

Having alienated his aides, it is also essential to alienate him from his own people.

13

Do not let him know our scheme, but lure him into our trap.

14

And then we will be able to accomplish our objectives.

15

Show kindness to the people, and do not begrudge the expense.

16

The people are like cattle and horses; feed them often and they will be obedient and close to you.

17

The mind is the means to acquire wisdom; wisdom generates wealth; wealth can nurture the people.

18

When a large number of virtuous people emerge, they can assist the monarch to rule the world."

CHAPTER III.

# DRAGON SECRET TEACHINGS

## THE KING'S WINGS

1

King Wu asked Taigong: "When a ruler leads an army, he must have a strong supporter to ensure extraordinary power. How does one achieve that?"

2

Taigong replied: "Whenever an army is raised, the fate of the army rests with the general.

3

To control the destiny of the army, it is most important for the general to know all aspects of the situation, and not to specialise in any particular skill.

4

Therefore, it is important to employ people according to their talents, to give full play to their strengths, to change them as the time comes, and to make it an institution.

5

That is why a general needs seventy-two assistants in order to follow the way of heaven.

6

He shall cope with various situations and employ assistants according to this method to master the rationale of being a general.

7

By bringing into play the singular talents of different people in different fields, all tasks can be successfully accomplished."

8

King Wu asked: "Would you elaborate?"

9

Taigong replied: "The most trusted assistant is mainly responsible for conspiring and planning to deal with sudden events, to observe celestial signs, to eliminate calamities, to take charge of military and political affairs, and to preserve the lives of the people.

10

Five advisers are mainly responsible for planning important events, considering the development of the situation, ascertaining the performances of the soldiers, declaring military discipline, granting various official positions, making decisions about difficult issues and deciding whether things are feasible.

11

Three astronomers are mainly responsible for observing the movement of the sun, moon and stars, measuring the wind and climate, calculating the auspiciousness of the times and days, examining the signs of fortune and misfortune, confirming the phenomena of disasters and investigating the allegiance of the people.

12

Three men are mainly responsible for identifying the terrain in which the army is to march and stay, analysing the advantages and disadvantages, observing the distances, the dangers and difficulties of the terrain, the water conditions of rivers and mountains, and ensuring that the army occupies favourable terrain.

13

Nine men are mainly responsible for discussing the similarities and differences between the enemy and us, analysing the reasons for victory and defeat in battle, monitoring the weapons used in battle, and denouncing all kinds of violations.

14

Four men are mainly responsible for planning supplies, preparing storage, ensuring the smooth flow of food transportation, collecting food and fodder for the army, and ensuring that the army does not experience difficulties in supply.

15

Four men are mainly responsible for selecting talented warriors, providing them with good weapons and equipment, and organising assault troops to move at speed and strike the enemy swiftly and quickly.

16

Three men are mainly responsible for the banners and drums of the army, making clear audio-visual signals, creating false symbols and issuing false orders to confuse the enemy, and coming and going in an unpredictable manner.

17

Four men are mainly responsible for carrying out important missions and arduous tasks and digging ditches and fortifications to prepare for the defence.

18

Three men are mainly responsible for improving on the deficiencies and making up for the faults of the generals, receiving guests, discussing problems, eliminating scourges and settling disputes.

19

Three men are mainly responsible for carrying out deceitful and unconventional schemes, setting up agendas to confuse the enemy, and constantly carrying out changes to the existing plans.

20

Seven men are mainly responsible for dealing with those from other states, observing their actions, finding out what is going on out there and understanding the enemy's situation.

21

Five men are mainly responsible for promoting the prestige of our army and inspiring the fighting spirit of the three armies, so that they will dare to take risks, attack and destroy the enemy without any fear.

22

Four men are mainly responsible for promoting the prestige of the general and commanders, so as to intimidate the distant regions, deter the neighbouring states and weaken the enemy's will.

23

Eight men are mainly responsible for detecting the enemy's agenda, spying on changes in the enemy state, manipulating the hearts and minds of the enemy, observing the enemy's intentions and conducting espionage.

24

Two men are mainly responsible for using trickery and the superstition of ghosts and spirits to convince our soldiers and stabilise the army.

25

Two men are mainly responsible for various kinds of medicine, healing wounds and curing diseases.

26

Two men are mainly responsible for calculating the income and expenditure of the army's camp, food and property."

# A DISCUSSION OF THE GENERAL

1

King Wu asked Taigong: "What are the principles for assessing a general?"

2

Taigong replied: "A general should possess five virtues and avoid ten flaws."

3

King Wu asked: "What do they refer to?"

4

Taigong said: "The five virtues of a general are: bravery, wisdom, kindness, integrity and fidelity.

5

If he is brave, he will not be violated; if he is wise, he will not be disturbed; if he is kind, he will love his soldiers; if he is honest, he will not deceive others; and if he is loyal, he will not betray.

6

The ten flaws are: brave but light on death, impatient and eager for success, covetous and greedy, merciful but appeasing, wise but timid and fearful, honest but gullible, incorruptible but mean to his men, wise but indecisive, strong but headstrong, cowardly and dependent on others.

7

He who is brave but light on death can be provoked to anger; he who is impatient and eager for success can be dragged down by a protracted war; he who is greedy and profit-seeking can be bribed with valuable goods; he who is kind but appease the enemy can be harassed and made to feel tired; he who is clever but timid can be intimidated; he who is honest but gullible can be deceived; he who is incorruptible but mean to his men can be insulted; he who is resourceful but indecisive can be attacked by surprise; he who is strong but headstrong can be entrapped, and he who is cowardly and likes to rely on others can be fooled.

8

Therefore, war is a matter of national importance, and whether a state exists or perishes is in the hands of its general.

9

A general, as the auxiliary of the state, has been valued by kings throughout history.

10

Therefore the appointment of the general shall be carefully scrutinised.

11

That is why it is said that: 'it is impossible to fight a war in which both sides are victorious or in which both sides are defeated.

12

As soon as one army ventures out beyond the border of the state, within ten days, either one side will perish or the other side will inevitably defeat the enemy and kill the enemy general.'"

13

King Wu said: "Excellent!"

# SELECTING THE GENERAL

1

King Wu asked Taigong: "When a king raises an army, he must choose men of both wisdom and courage to be his general and commanders. What is the best way to know the character and ability of these men?"

2

Taigong replied: "There are fifteen cases in which the appearance of a man does not match his true character: some appear to be wise but are not; some appear to be kind but are engaged in theft and plunder; some appear to be modest but are arrogant; some appear to be clean but are not sincere; some appear to be competent but are not really talented; some appear to be loyal but are dishonest; some appear to be wise but are indecisive; some appear to be decisive but are inactive, some appear to be honest but are untrustworthy; some appear to be wavering but are loyal; some appear to be aggressive but are effective; some appear to be brave but are timid; some appear to be serious but are approachable; some appear to be stern but are gentle and generous; some appear to be frail and ugly but are able to do everything they are told to do.

3

Those who are despised by the common men are often held in high esteem by the sages.

4

The common men cannot understand this, nor can they see through the appearance without great insight.

5

These are the various cases in which appearance does not match inner qualities."

6

King Wu asked: "By what means can we truly understand them?"

7

Taigong replied: "There are eight ways to understand them: first, to ask questions and see how they respond; second, to question them in detail to see how well they respond; third, to examine them through spies to see if they are loyal; fourth, to ask them knowingly to see if they are hiding anything, so as to examine their character; fifth, to let them manage wealth to see if they are honest and not greedy; sixth, to test them with women to see if they have strong willpower; seventh, to ask them to handle a crisis to see if they are brave; and eighth, to make them drunk to see if they behave. After these eight methods have been applied, it will be possible to tell whether a man is virtuous or unworthy."

## APPOINTING THE GENERAL

1

King Wu asked Taigong: "What is the ceremony for appointing a general?"

2

Taigong replied: "Whenever the state is in danger, the king avoids the main hall and summons the general in a side hall and gives him an edict: 'The safety of the state rests on the general. A certain state is now in rebellion, and the general is to lead an army to conquer it.'

3

After the general has received the order, the king orders the chief history scribe to perform divination, then fasts for three days, goes to the ancestral temple, reads the signs given by the divination, and chooses an auspicious day accordingly to award the battle-axe to the general. On the auspicious day, the ruler enters the gate of the Imperial Temple and stand facing west; the general then enters the gate of the Imperial Temple and stands facing north.

4

The king himself takes the upper part of the battle-axe and hands its handle to the general, declaring: 'From now on, all matters of the army from this up to heaven are at the disposal of the general.' Then he takes the handle of the axe and confers the blade to the general, declaring: 'Henceforth, all matters in the army from this to the depths below are at the general's disposal. Advance when you see the enemy weak, and stop when you see them strong; do not think that our army is large and despise the enemy; do not risk your life because the task is great; do not despise your men because you are honourable; do not think that you have unique opinions and go against the wishes of the people; do not think that you are right because you are eloquent.

5

Do not sit down before your soldiers sit down; do not eat before your soldiers eat; share heat and cold with your men.

6

In this way, the soldiers will fight with all their might.' When the general accepts his appointment, he replies: 'I have heard that the affairs of state must not be interfered with from outside, and that battles cannot be commanded by the monarch from the court.

7

If a minister is disloyal, he cannot serve his ruler faithfully, and if a general is under the control of his ruler and has many doubts, he cannot concentrate on the enemy.

8

Since I have been ordered to take charge of the military, I dare not return until I have won.

9

I hope that Your Majesty will grant complete and sole command to, but if you do not, I dare not take on this responsibility.'

10

When the king gives his permission, the general leaves the king to lead the army.

11

From then on, all the affairs of the army are under the command of the general, not of the king.

12

When he fights the enemy, he can concentrate on his efforts because there are no distractions.

13

In this way, the general is able to lead his troops into battle without the constraints of heaven and earth, without the enemy daring to resist him and without the king interfering with him.

14

Thus, the wise and resourceful men are willing to advise and the brave men willing to fight and kill, and the morale will be so high that the army will act as swift as a galloping horse, and the enemy will be subdued before the battle is even fought.

15

When war is won outside the court and merit is established within it, officials are promoted; soldiers are rewarded; the common people rejoice, and the general is not punished for his faults.

16

Thus, the winds and the rains are favourable; the grains are plentiful; and the state is at peace."

17

King Wu said: "Excellent!"

# THE GENERAL'S AUTHORITY

1

King Wu asked Taigong: "What methods should a general employ to establish his authority? By what means should a general demonstrate righteousness and wisdom? By what means are prohibitions to be implemented and orders to be carried out?"

2

Taigong replied: "A general establishes prestige by killing those of high rank, and demonstrates righteousness and wisdom by rewarding those of low rank; and by punishing and rewarding clearly, prohibitions are always implemented and orders are always carried out.

3

Thus, if one man is killed and the whole army will be shocked, kill him; if one man is rewarded and the whole army will be happy, reward him.

4

The focus of execution should be on those of high rank, while the focus of reward should be on those of low rank.

5

The punishment reaches the top of the hierarchy by killing those who hold important positions of authority, while the reward for those of low status, such as cattlemen, horsemen and breeders, reach the bottom of the hierarchy.

6

The fact that the punishment reaches the top and the reward reaches the bottom is why the general's authority is established and his orders are carried out."

## ENCOURAGING THE ARMY

1

King Wu asked Taigong: "I would like to see the three armies compete to be the first to ascend a city during a siege and to charge in a field battle; they become angry when they hear the call to retreat, and rejoice when they hear the call to march. How can I achieve this?"

2

Taigong replied: "There are three essential factors for a general to crush his enemy."

3

King Wu asked: "What do they refer to?"

4

Taigong said: "A general who can go without a leather coat in winter, without a fan in summer, and without an umbrella in the rain is called a courteous general; a general who cannot set an example in these conditions will have no way to appreciate how cold and hot his soldiers feel.

5

When crossing a dangerous pass or a muddy road, a general must first dismount his chariot and horse and walk; then he is considered a strong general.

6

If a general does not set an example, he will not be able to appreciate the hardships of his soldiers. Only after the camp where the army is stationed has been arranged does the general return to his own to rest, and only after the soldiers' meal is ready does the general begin to eat.

7

A general who does not set up a fire to illuminate his army is a suppressive general.

8

A general who cannot restrain his appetite has no way to appreciate the hunger of his soldiers.

9

If a general is able to share his soldiers' hunger and satiety, then the whole army will rejoice when they hear the call to advance and become angry when they hear the call to stop.

10

When attacking a fortified city, even when faced with a hail of arrows and stones, soldiers will fight to be the first to scale the city wall; even when blades clash, soldiers will be the first to fight.

11

It is not the soldiers' natural inclination to die or to be maimed, but if the generals cares for their warmth and hunger, and is sympathetic to their sufferings, they will be moved to serve."

## SECRET TALLIES

1

King Wu asked Taigong: "When our army is deep into the territory of an enemy state and the whole army encounters an emergency, which is either to our advantage or detriment, what should we do if we decide to inform the home state to assist the three armies?"

2

Taigong replied: "There are eight kinds of secret military tallies granted by the sovereign to his generals: there is the tally for our army to win a great victory and wipe out the enemy's army, which is one *chi** in length; there is the tally for breaking the enemy's army and capturing the enemy's general, which is nine *cun** in length; there is the tally for forcing the enemy's army to surrender and capturing the enemy's city, which is eight *cun* in length; there is the tally for repelling the enemy and informing them of the battle, which is seven *cun* in length; there is the tally for inspiring the army and the people to be strong, which is six *cun* in length; there is the tally for requesting supplies of food and reinforcements, which is five *cun* in lengths; there is the tally for reporting the defeat of an army and the death of a general, which is four *cun* in length; there is the tally for reporting the defeat of a battle and the death of a soldier, which is three *cun* in length.

3

For those who are instructed to pass on a secret tally but delay the time, divulge secrets, overhear and casually pass on information shall all be punished with death.

*chi is a traditional Chinese unit of measurement that is about 0.32m.
*cun is a traditional Chinese unit of measurement that is about 0.032m.

4

These eight types of tallies, held in secret by the monarch and the general, are a means of communication used to deliver messages in secret without revealing imperial and battlefield secrets. In so doing, even if the enemy are highly intelligent, they will not be able to decipher their meanings."

5

King Wu said: "Brilliant!"

## SECRET LETTERS

1

King Wu asked Taigong: "When our army is deep into the territory of an enemy state, the general and I would like to gather the forces and manoeuvre flexibly according to the enemy's situation, seeking to win by surprise.

2

But the matter is so complicated that it is difficult to explain with a secret tally, and the distance between my army and me is so great that words are difficult to communicate.

3

What should be done in such a situation?"

4

Taigong replied: "All secret plots should be made with a secret letter, not a secret tally.

5

The ruler uses the letter to convey instructions to the general, and the general uses the letter to ask the ruler for advice.

6

It is supposed to be a combination of three parts with three messengers to deliver.

7

The letter shall be divided into three parts and three people are sent to deliver the letter, each of them only carries a part of the letter; even the person who delivers the letter does not know its content.

8

In so doing, no matter how clever the enemy are, they will not be able to find out our secret."

9

King Wu said: "Excellent!"

# THE ARMY'S STRATEGIC POWER

1

King Wu asked Taigong: "What are the principles of offensive combat?"

2

Taigong replied: "The situation of combat is determined by the actions of the enemy; the changes in tactics arise from the confrontation between the enemy and us; and the use of regular and ad-hoc tactics comes from the infinite wisdom and thinking of the general.

3

Therefore, the most important secrets must not be divulged, and the tactics of using the army must not be passed on in words.

4

Moreover, secrets are extremely important and can only be hidden in the heart but not expressed as arguments, and the deployment and use of the army can only be concealed but not exposed to the enemy.

5

This is the principle of using the army, which is to move swiftly and strike suddenly, and to act without being subjected to any constraint.

6

When the enemy hear that our troops are marching, they will discuss their response; when the enemy find out what our troops are doing, they will devise a plan against us; when the enemy understand our intentions, our troops will be in trouble; when the enemy understand our plans, our troops will be in danger.

7

Therefore, those who are good at using the army are able to win before the army is used; those who are good at eliminating scourges are able to eliminate them before they happen; those who are good at winning battles are able to win them invisibly.

8

The most brilliant warfare is that which brings the enemy to their knees without fighting.

9

Therefore, he who wins a battle by fighting to death is not a good general; he who sets up defence after a defeat is not a wise general; he who is as wise as the average man cannot be called a sage; he who is as skilled as the average man cannot be called a master.

10

There is nothing more important in the use of army than to conquer all attacks; nothing more important in battle than to keep secrets; nothing more important in action than to surprise, and nothing more important in planning than to be unpredictable.

11

Where victory is achieved before battle, it is attained by first showing weakness to the enemy and then engaging in a decisive battle.

12

In this way, one can get twice the result with half the effort.

13

Sages observe the changes in heaven and earth and repeatedly seek the laws of their operation.

14

They deduce the universal law of change based on the movement of the sun and moon, the change of seasons, and the length of day and night.

15

The life and death of all things depend on the changes of heaven and earth.

16

Therefore, if a man fights without understanding the situation of war, he is bound to fail even when he has a large army.

17

Those who are good at commanding battles do not get distracted by illusions, and when they see a certainty of victory, they attack, but when there is no possibility of victory, they stop.

18

Therefore, do not be afraid and do not hesitate. The greatest harm in using the army is hesitation; the greatest disaster to the army is doubt.

19

Those who are good at war never let go of a favourable situation when they see it, and never hesitate when they encounter an opportunity to strike.

20

Otherwise, they will suffer calamities.

21

Therefore, a wise general will not let go of an opportunity when he seizes it and will never hesitate once he has made his decision.

22

This is why the battle shall be fought like a thunderbolt strikes. Who can defeat such an army when those who stand in its way are crushed and those who approach it are destroyed?

23

When a general uses his troops, he who is able to be calm and confident is called a god; and he who has insight before the situation is known is called a sage.

24

Therefore, when one has mastered the truth of being a god and sage, he will not have opponents in battle, and no enemy state will dare to oppose him."

25

King Wu said: "Excellent!"

# THE UNORTHODOX ARMY

1

King Wu asked Taigong: "What is the key to the use of the army?"

2

Taigong replied: "In antiquity, those who were good at using the army were not so marvellous that they were omnipotent; their success all depended on whether they could make things unpredictable.

3

Those who could were victorious, and those who could not were defeated.

4

When two armies are facing each other, the purpose of unloading armour, laying down arms, indulging soldiers and disorganising ranks is to lure the enemy by deception; the purpose of occupying grassy areas is to facilitate a concealed retreat; the purpose of occupying treacherous terrain in valleys is to fight a large number of men with few; the purpose of occupying low, wet and dark areas is to prevent the enemy from moving in chariots and cavalry; the purpose of occupying treacherous mountainous terrain is to conceal the movement of the army; the purpose of occupying flat and open areas is to match the enemy's courage and strength.

5

To move as fast as a flying arrow in order to break the enemy's sophisticated and clever plans with a swift move; to set up clever ambushes and surprise troops to disrupt the enemy's round and square formations; to take advantage of the enemy's panic to launch an attack in order to strike ten with one; to take advantage of the enemy's fatigue and night camping to carry out a surprise attack in order to strike a hundred with ten; to use marvellous techniques to build bridges and boats in order to cross deep water; to use solid crossbows and long weapons in order to make it easier to fight across the water; to set up checkpoints in remote areas, send out ad-hoc forces and move quickly and unconventionally in order to subdue enemy cities and occupy enemy lands; to deliberately advance with loud noises and drumbeats in order to confuse the enemy and carry out unorthodox and clever strategies; to operate in windy and stormy weather in order to attack from various directions; to pretend to be an emissary of the enemy and sneak in behind the enemy in order to cut off the their food routes; to use the enemy's orders and dress in their costumes in order to prepare for retreat; to give the officers and soldiers a clear explanation in battle in order to inspire them to overcome the enemy; to confer titles and rewards in order to encourage them to serve bravely; to impose severe punishments in order to encourage tired officers and soldiers to persevere in battle; to strike a balance between pleasure and anger, reward and punishment, courtesy and authority and fast and slow in order to unify the mindset and actions of the men; to occupy high and open terrain in order to facilitate vigilance and guarding; to hold on to the dangerous passages in order to strengthen defence; to occupy deep and wooded terrain in order to conceal the movement of the army; to dig deep trenches, build high barriers and store sufficient supplies in order to sustain the battle.

6

Therefore, if one does not know the strategy of attack, one cannot fight against the enemy; if one does not know how to use the troops, one cannot win by surprise; if one does not know how to crack down on the chaos of the army, one cannot adapt to the situation.

7

Therefore, if the general is not kind, the army will not support him; if the general is not brave, the army will not be able to fight; if the general is not wise, the army will be suspicious; if the general is not a strategist, the army will be defeated; if the general does not think carefully, the army will lose the opportunity to fight; if the general is not vigilant, the army will be negligent; if the general is not strong in leadership, the army will be lax. Therefore, the general is the master of the army.

8

If the general is disciplined, the army will be disciplined with him; if the general is incompetent, the army will be in chaos.

9

If you have a wise and competent general, your state will prosper and your army will be strong; if you do not have a wise and competent general, your state will crumble and your army will perish."

10

King Wu said: "Excellent!"

## THE FIVE NOTES

1

King Wu asked Taigong: "Can you judge the strength of an army and predict the victory or defeat of a war from the sound and music of their pitch pipes?"

2

Taigong replied: "Your Majesty's question is profound! There are twelve notes in a pitch pipe, of which five are the main ones, namely, Do, Re, Mi, So and La.

3

These five are the most fundamental notes. And they will remain unchanged for thousands of generations.

4

These five notes can be likened to the five elements as the natural laws of the heaven and the earth, and can be used to predict changes in the enemy's situation.

5

Each of the five elements – gold, wood, water, fire and earth – operates by the interplay of the five.

6

Likewise, the way to use the military is also to use the five notes to win and attack the invincible! In antiquity, the Three Emperors revered the art of rule with inaction to restrain violence.

7

There was no writing back then, and everything was done according to the five elements.

8

The principle that the five elements are mutually exclusive is the natural law of the evolution of heaven and earth, just as the subtle changes of celestial signs.

9

When the weather is clear and sunny and there are no clouds or rain, the general shall send horsemen to nine hundred steps away from the enemy's camp in the middle of the night.

10

The soldiers shall hold pitch pipes to their ears and shout at the enemy to startle them.

11

At this point, an echo from the enemy's side will be heard through the pipe, which is very faint.

12

If the sound of a Mi is echoed in the pipe, the enemy should be attacked from the west, a direction represented by White Tiger; if the sound of a So is echoed in the pipe, the enemy should be attacked from the north, a direction represented by Turtle; if the sound of a Re is echoed in the pipe, the enemy should be attacked from the south, a direction represented by Vermilion Bird; if the sound of a La is echoed in the pipe, the enemy should be attacked from the centre, a direction represented by Hook Star.

13

If there is no echo in the pipe, then it implies the sound of Do; so the enemy should be attacked from the east, a direction represented by Green Dragon.

14

All these are the fulfilment of the five elements, which are signs that complement the victory and the key to success."
King Wu said: "Excellent!"

15

Taigong said: "The subtle sounds and rhythms all have external signs."

16

King Wu asked: "By what means can we truly understand them?"

17

Taigong said: "Listen carefully when the enemy are alarmed: their drumbeats imply the sound of Mi; the light of fire, the sound of So; the noises of various weapons of iron spears and halberds, the sound of Re; screaming, the sound of La, and silence, the sound of Do. Each of these five notes is consistent with the movements of the outside world."

## THE ARMY'S INDICATIONS

1

King Wu asked Taigong: "What should I do if I want to know the enemy's strength and weakness and foresee the indications of victory or defeat in war before the battle is fought?"

2

Taigong replied: "The indications of victory and defeat are first manifested in the enemy's spirit.

3

A wise general will be able to detect them, but whether or not one can use them to defeat the enemy depends on one's efforts. Observe the enemy's movements, the good and bad omens that are spoken of and the things that the soldiers talk about.

4

If the whole army is happy; if the soldiers fear the law and respect the orders of the general, if they are happy to have defeated the enemy; if they are proud of each other's bravery and might, this is a indication that the army is strong in battle.

5

If the whole army is constantly alarmed; if the soldiers are scattered and disorganised; if they are intimidated by the strength of the enemy; if they spread rumours of the battle; if they argue among themselves; if they cannot stop the rumours; if they agitate and deceive each other; if they do not fear the law; and if they do not respect the general and each other, this is an indication that the army is weak in battle.

6

When the army is in unison; the formation is strong; the ditch is deep and the fortification is high; with the favourable weather conditions of strong wind and rain the three armies can charge forward without orders; and when the sound of gongs and drums is loud and clear, this is an indication that the army has the help of the gods and will win a great victory.

7

However, when the formation is unstable; the flags are disorderly and the direction is unclear; and against the unfavourable weather conditions of strong wind and rain, the army is in a state of confusion; when the soldiers are terrified and fearful; their morale is depleted and disorganised, the horses are frightened and disorganised, the chariots are broken, and the sound of gongs and drums is dull and depressing, this is an indication of a great defeat for the army.

8

Whenever a city is attacked and besieged: if the energy flow above the city is of a deadly colour, the city may be destroyed; if the energy flow goes out to the north, the city may be captured; if it goes out and flows to the west, the city may surrender; if it goes out and flows to the south, the city stands firm; if it goes out and flows to the east, the city cannot be attacked; if the it goes out comes back, the defender of the city must flee and be defeated; if it rises and covers our army, our army will be disadvantaged; if the it rises high and does not stop, the battle will last for a long time.

9

If it does not thunder and rain after ten days, the siege must be quickly withdrawn, for there must be a wise and able support in the city. In this way, you will know why you should attack when you can, and stop when you cannot."

10

King Wu said: "Excellent!"

# AGRICULTURAL IMPLEMENTS

1

King Wu asked Taigong: "When the world is stable and there is no war in the state, can we not prepare instruments for battles and sieges? Can we not prepare the facilities for defence against the enemy?"

2

Taigong replied: "The equipment for attacking and defending in times of war is in fact all in the tools of production and livelihood used by the people in peaceful times. Ploughs can be used as obstacles such as caltrops and chevaux de frise; ox carts can be used as barriers such as barricades and shields; agricultural tools such as hoes and harrows can be used as spears and halberds; straw raincoats, umbrellas and hats can be used as armour and shelters; shovels, axes, saws, mortars and pestles can be used as siege equipment; oxen and horses can be used to transport food; chickens and dogs can be used to tell the time and alarm; cloth and silk spun by women can be used to make battle flags.

## 3

In spring, the method of cutting grass and removing thorns can be used as a technique for fighting the enemy's chariots and cavalry; in summer, the method of ploughing the fields and hoeing the grass can be used as a technique for fighting the enemy's infantry; in autumn, the harvesting of crops and fodder can be used as food and fodder for war; in winter, food piled up in warehouses can be used to prepare for a long defensive period in times of war.

## 4

People of the same village can be grouped together in units of five soldiers, which are the basis for the formation and management of the army in times of war; villages shall have governors who act as officers of the army in time of war; walls are built between villages, which cannot be crossed and function as the distinction of the army's quarters in time of war; the transport of grain and the harvesting of food can guarantee the army's reserves in time of war; the construction of the city and the ditches in spring and autumn are the same as the construction of the walls and ditches in time of war.

5

Thus, the tools of warfare are ubiquitous in the ordinary life of agricultural production. Anyone who is good at governing a state attaches great importance to agriculture.

6

Therefore, it is necessary to make the people breed their animals, cultivate their fields and settle their dwellings, so that men can cultivate a certain number of farmlands and women can weave a certain amount of cloth.

7

This is the way to enrich the state and strengthen the army."

8

King Wu said: "Excellent!"

CHAPTER IV.

# TIGER SECRET TEACHINGS

# THE ARMY'S EQUIPMENT

1

King Wu asked Taigong: "When a king raises an army for battle, is there a certain standard for distinguishing the types of armaments and the number of equipment of attack and defence?"

2

Taigong replied: "Your Majesty are indeed asking a complicated question! There are different types and numbers of offensive and defensive instruments, and this is a major issue concerning the strength of the army."

3

King Wu said: "I would like to hear the details."

4

Taigong said: "Whenever an army of ten thousand men is used in battle, there is a general standard of weaponry: thirty-six chariots called Wu Chong Da Fu Xu.

5

They are guarded by skilled and brave warriors using strong crossbows, spears and halberds, each chariot being pushed by twenty-four men.

6

The height of the wheels is eight *chi*, and the chariots are equipped with banners and drums.

7

In the art of war, this chariot is called a shocking chariot, and it can be used to break through a hard line and defeat a strong enemy.

8

There are seventy-two chariots, known as the Wu Yi Da Lu Mao Ji Fu Xu.

9

They are guarded by skilled and brave warriors using powerful crossbows, spears and halberds on both sides.

10

Their wheels are five *chi* high and are equipped with crossbows that are fired from a winch, so that they can be used to break through a strong formation and defeat a powerful enemy.

11

There are one hundred and fourty chariots called Ti Yi Xiao Lu Fu Xu.

12

They are equipped with winch-fired crossbows and ride on a single wheel and can be used to break through a formidable line and defeat a powerful enemy.

13

There are thirty-six chariots called Da Huang Can Lian Wan Da Fu Xu.

14

They are guarded by skilled and brave warriors using powerful crossbows, spears and halberds, and are accompanied by two kinds of arrows known as Fei Fu and Dian Ying.

15

Fei Fu has a red pole with white feathers and a bronze head, while Dian Ying has a green pole with red feathers and an iron head.

16

During the day, a large red silk is used as the banner, which is six *chi* long and six *cun* wide, and is called Glorious; at night, a white silk is used as the banner, which is six *chi* long and six *cun* wide, and is called Shooting Star.

17

This chariot can be used to break through formations and defeat powerful enemies.

18

There are thirty-six chariots, known as Da Fu Xu. They carry warriors nicknames as mantis; they can be used to attack and defeat the enemy.

19

There are chariots known as Zi Che Kou Ji or Dian Che.

20

They can be used to break through a fortified line and defeat the enemy's foot soldiers.

21

When the enemy come in the dark, it is advisable to use one hundred and sixty chariots called Mao Ji Fu Xu, each carrying three mantis warriors.

22

This is known in military art as the Thunder Strike.

23

This chariot can be used to break through formations and defeat powerful enemies.

24

There are one thousand and two hundred iron rods called Fang Shou; each weighs twelve *jin** and has handles over five *chi* long. They are also called Tian Bang.

25

There are one thousand and two hundred long-handled axes called Da Ke; each has a blade eight *cun* long and a handle five *chi* long and weighs eight *jin*.

26

They are also called Tian Yue. There are one thousand and two hundred square-headed iron mallets; each weighs eight *jin* with a handle of five *chi* long.

27

All these weapons could be used to defeat the enemy's foot soldiers.

*jin is a traditional Chinese unit of mass that is equivalent to around 604 grams.

28

There are one thousand and two hundred flying hooks; each is eight *cun* long with a four-cun long tip and a shank over six *chi* long; they can be thrown to wound the enemy.

29

As for the defence, there are one hundred and twenty of Mu Tang Lang Jian Ren Fu Xu; each one is two *zhang** wide.

30

They are known as chevaux de frise.

31

On flat, open terrain, the infantry can use them to impede the movement of enemy chariots and horses.

*zhang is a traditional Chinese unit of measurement that is about 3.2m long.

32

There are one hundred and twenty caltrops that should be set two *chi* and five *cun* above the ground.

33

They are used to impede the movement of the enemy's infantry, to stop an exhausted enemy, and to intercept a retreating and fleeing enemy.

34

There are one hundred and twenty chariots, known as Zhou Xuan Duan Chong Mao Ji Fu Xu. There were onced deployed by the Yellow Emperor to defeat Chiyou.

35

They can also be used to disrupt the enemy's infantry, to stop the exhausted enemy and to intercept the retreating enemy.

36

Caltrops can be placed on narrow roads and paths.

37

They are four *cun* long and eight *cun* wide and over six *chi* long; there are a total of one thousand and two hundred of them.

38

They can be used to hinder the movement of the enemy's infantry.

39

When the enemy come suddenly in the darkness of the night and the battle is fierce, it is time to set up the trap by laying two lines of one thousand and two hundred caltrops and obstacles, each with two *cun* apart.

40

In the wilderness and in deep grass, one thousand and two hundred obstacles should be placed. They are one *chi* and five *cun* above the ground.

41

They are used to defeat the enemy's infantry and horses, to stop the exhausted enemy, and to intercept a retreating enemy.

42

On narrow paths and low-lying terrain, a hundred and twenty obstacles called iron-armed locks should be erected.

43

They are used to defeat the enemy's infantry and horses, to stop the exhausted enemy, and to intercept a retreating enemy.

44

To guard the camp gates, twelve spears, halberds and small sculls are used, and a winch with a series of crossbows is attached.

45

When the army is on the defensive, it should set up one hundred and twenty barriers; each one is one *zhang* and five *chi* wide and eight *chi* high.

46

Also set up five hundred and twenty chariots; each one is also one *zhang* long and five *chi* wide and eight *chi* high.

47

To cross ditches and valleys, eight flying bridges shall be set up; each one is one *zhang* and five *chi* wide and more than two *zhang* long, equipped with a turning windlass and erected with iron rings and long ropes.

48

To cross rivers, eight floating bridges shall be set up; each one is one *zhang* and five *chi* wide and more than two *zhang* long and with iron rings and long ropes to link them together.

49

Thirty-two pontoons with iron anchors shall be set up; each one is round inside and over four *chi* long outside, and is linked by iron rings and ropes.

50

By using the pontoons to set up the floating bridges, it is likely to cross a large river.

51

This kind of river-crossing contraption is called Tian Huang, also known as Tian Chuan.

52

When the army camp in wilderness, they shall use timber to form fences called Hu Luo Chai Ying.

53

There are one thousand and two hundred of them that are linked by long ropes with iron rings; each one is more than two *zhang* long.

54

For those six hundred thick ropes with iron rings, the rings are four *cun* in size and the ropes over four *zhang* long.

55

For those three hundred medium ropes with iron rings, the rings are two *cun* in size and the ropes over four *zhang* long.

56

For those twelve thousand short ropes, each one is over two *zhang* long.

57

When it rains, chariots shall be covered with boards, which are grooved to fit the wagons; each board is four *chi* wide and over four *zhang* long. There shall be one board for each chariot and it is fastened with nails.

58

There are three hundred great axes for felling trees, each weighing eight *jin* with a handle more than three *chi* long.

59

There are three hundred great hoes called Qi Jue; each has a blade six *cun* wide and a handle more than five *chi* long.

60

There are three great hammers called Tong Zhu Gu; each is more than five *chi* long. There are three hundred iron rakes called Ying Zhao Fang Xiong; each has a handle more than seven *chi* long.

61

There are three hundred forked poles called Fang Xiong Tie Cha; each has a handle more than seven *chi* long.

62

There are three hundred large sickles for cutting herbs; each has a shank over seven *chi* long. There are three hundred grass-cutting tools called Da Lu; each weighs eight *jin* with a shank six *chi* long.

63

There are three hundred iron pegs with rings; each is over three *chi* long.

64

There are one hundred and twenty large iron mallets for nailing pegs; each weighs five *jin* with a shank over two *chi* long.

65

For an army of ten thousand men, it is essential to have six thousand crossbows, two thousand sets of halberds and shields, two thousand sets of spears and shields, and three hundred skilled craftsmen to repair the instruments of war and make weapons.

66

These are the approximate numbers of equipment needed to raise an army of ten thousand for battle."

67

King Wu said: "That is true!"

## THREE FORMATIONS

1

King Wu asked Taigong: "What is the Heaven Formation, Earth Formation and Human Formation for war?"

2

Taigong replied: "To set up a formation according to the specific position of the sun, moon, stars and the Big Dipper is the Heaven Formation; to set up a formation based on the terrain conditions such as hills, mountains, water and ponds is the Earth Formation; to set up a formation in accordance with the types of soldiers such as chariot soldiers, cavalry and different battle methods such as political entrapping or taking by force is the Human Formation."

3

King Wu said: "Excellent!"

# URGENT BATTLES

1

King Wu asked Taigong: "If the enemy surround our army, cutting off our retreat routes as well as the routes for food transportation, what should we do in such a situation?"

2

Taigong replied: "This is the most difficult situation. A quick breakout would lead to victory, but a hesitant move would lead to defeat.

3

The way to break out of the siege is to set up the troops in a fourfold battle formation with guards on all sides; use powerful chariots and brave cavalry to shock the enemy's army and cause confusion among them, and then quickly assault them so that we can break out unhindered."

4

King Wu asked: "If our army has successfully broken out of the siege and still wants to take advantage of the situation to defeat the enemy army, what should we do?"

5

Taigong replied: "We should quickly attack the enemy's left flank with our left army and the enemy's right flank with our right army; do not fight for paths to avoid scattering our troops. At the same time, use our central army to attack the enemy in turn, either by striking their front or their rear. In so doing, the enemy can be defeated despite their large size."

## CERTAIN ESCAPE

1

King Wu asked Taigong: "If the enemy surround our army, cutting off our retreat routes as well as the routes for food transportation, and they outnumber us and have an abundance of food supplies, what should we do in such a situation?"

2

Taigong replied: "To break out of the enemy's siege, weapons and equipment are vital, but fighting bravely is paramount.

3

If you carefully identify the enemy's weaknesses and unguarded locations and take advantage of their weaknesses, you can definitely break out of the siege. The strategy for breaking out is to move in the dark with black banners, weapons in hand and muzzles on mouth.

4

Make the brave and strong, flexible and daring soldiers the vanguard to capture certain enemy strongholds and open the way for our army; ask the skilled and brave warriors to use strong crossbows and act as ambush forces, hiding behind to cover the movement of the main forces; make the old and weak soldiers and chariots and horses march in between.

5

Once deployed, move calmly and cautiously without panic. Use the chariots called Wu Chong Fu Xu to escort the front and rear, and the chariots called Wu Yi Da Lu to cover the left and right.

6

If the enemy detect our breakthrough, our brave and powerful vanguard shall quickly charge forward, followed by old and weak soldiers and chariots, while skilled warriors equipped with strong crossbows shall lie in ambush.

7

When the enemy come in pursuit of our army, our ambush forces shall quickly attack their flanks and rear, and use fire and drums in abundance to confuse the enemy, so that they will feel as if our army has emerged from the ground and descends from the sky, and the whole army will fight bravely, and the enemy will not be able to stop our breakthrough."

8

King Wu asked: "If there is a big river, a wide valley or a deep pit in front of us, and our army has to cross over but is not prepared with boats, what should we do in such a situation when the enemy have fortified their troops to stop our advance and block our retreat; when their scouts are on guard; when they have occupied all the dangerous terrain; when their chariots and cavalry are blocking in front, and when their warriors are attacking from behind?"

9

Taigong replied: "Where there are large rivers, wide valleys and deep ditches, the enemy will not normally put up defences.

10

Even if they are fortified, they must not deploy a large number of soldiers. Therefore, our troops can be ferried across using such tools as the flying bridges, windlasses and pontoons.

11

Send brave warriors in the designated direction to charge and fight to the death and then burn our chariots and food to tell all our men clearly that to fight bravely is to survive and to cower and fight timidly is to die.

12

Once already out of danger, let our advance guard set up smoke and fire signals, send scouts, and occupy jungles, graves and treacherous terrain.

13

In this way, the enemy's chariots and cavalry must not dare to drive long distances after us.

14

The purpose of setting up smoke and fire signals is to direct the advance guard to gather in a place where there is fire.

15

The enemy will not be able to stop our army if all our soldiers are sharp and brave enough to fight."

16

King Wu said: "Excellent!"

## PLANNING FOR THE ARMY

1

King Wu asked Taigong: "When our troops are deep into the enemy's territory, we encounter deep streams, large valleys and rivers that are difficult to cross. Before we can fully cross the rivers, heavy rain falls, floods come and the water level rises sharply, and the rest of our troops behind are cut off by the water with no boats, bridges, or supplies. Under such circumstances, what should be done to get the whole army across, so that it will not be stranded for too long?"

2

Taigong replied: "Whenever you lead an army into battle, if plans are not made in advance; if equipment is not prepared in advance; if training is not put into practice, and if soldiers are not skilled, the the army will not win.

3

Whenever there is a major military operation, there is no army that does not train its soldiers to be skilled in the use of various instruments.

4

For example, when siegeing a city, our army shall use various chariots to launch an offensive; when observing the enemy inside the city, we shall use ladders and flying towers to watch the enemy's movements; when our three armies are advancing and stationed, we shall use chariots to cover for the front and back; when cutting off traffic and blocking the streets, we shall send brave and skilled soldiers to control both sides with strong crossbows; when setting up a camp, we shall place obstacles.

5

When it is daytime, we shall climb the ladders to watch over the enemy.

6

At night, fireworks shall be lit; thunder drums shall be beaten; drums shall be hit; bells shall be shaken, and pipes shall be blown as a command signal.

7

As for crossing ditches and valleys, flying bridges, turnstiles and windlasses shall be used; as for crossing large rivers, boats shall be used; as for travelling against the current, floating contraptions shall be used.

8

When the three armies have all the equipment they need, what worries does the general have?"

# APPROACHING THE BORDER

1

King Wu asked Taigong: "When our army and the enemy are facing each other at the border, the enemy can come and attack us, and we can go forward and attack the enemy. Both sides are in a strong position, but neither dares to take the lead. If we want to go forward and attack the enemy, but are afraid that the enemy will strike back, what should be done?"

2

Taigong replied: "In this case, divide our army into three parts: front, middle and rear.

3

Order the front army to dig deep ditches and fortify high walls, and not to go into battle.

4

The rear army is told to gather more food so that the enemy will not know our intentions.

5

Then, send our best troops to assault the centre of the enemy troops unexpectedly.

6

As a result, the enemy will be unable to understand the situation of our army and will stop moving and dare not come to attack."

7

King Wu asked: "What if the enemy are aware of our situation and intentions, and as soon as our army moves, the enemy know our next step and therefore send their elite troops to ambush us in deep grass, to intercept us, and to attack where our defences are inadequate?"

8

Taigong replied: "Order our front troops to go forth on a daily basis to challenge the enemy, in order to wear down and slacken their spirit; order our old and weak soldiers to drag branches, raise dust, beat drums and shout, and run back and forth to make a noise.

9

When the challenge is made, send the troops either on the enemy's left or right side and not more than a hundred steps from them.

10

With our constant harassment, the enemy's general will be drained and the enemy's soldiers will be terrified.

11

As a result, the enemy will not dare to attack our army.

12

Then, if our army keeps the momentum of assaulting the enemy either from inside or outside, our whole army will be swiftly engaged in battle, and the enemy will certainly be defeated."

## MOVEMENT AND REST

1

King Wu asked Taigong: "When our army is deep into the territory of an enemy state, and the enemy and us are evenly matched.

2

In this situation, we want to make the enemy's general fearful, their troops demoralised, their formation unstable, their rear soldiers trying to escape and the front line wavering.

3

Then what should be done to beat the drums and shout and take advantage of the situation to trounce the enemy?"

4

Taigong replied: "To do this, we must send troops to a place ten lis behind the enemy and ambush on both sides of the road; then send chariots and cavalry a hundred lis further out to the far rear of the enemy's army, and order the troops to prepare more flags and set up more gongs and drums.

5

When the battle between the two sides is launched, beat the drums and shout, and all our troops will attack the enemy at the same time. In this way, the enemy's general and soldiers will be terrified, so that they cannot rescue one another and the officers cannot look after each other. Consequently, the enemy's army will surely fail."

6

King Wu asked: "What if the enemy are in a terrain that does not allow us to set up ambush on either side of them; our chariots and cavalry cannot go around to the enemy's far rear; at the same time they are aware of our intentions and have prepared well in advance; our soldiers are pessimistic and despondent; and our general is fearful and cannot win? What should we do in such a situation?"

7

Taigong replied: "Your Majesty are asking a complicated question! In such a case, we shall send out scouts from afar five days before the battle to spy on the enemy, to check for signs that the enemy are coming, and to set up ambushes beforehand to await their advance.

8

The enemy must be engaged on the most unfavourable terrain for them.

9

We shall scatter our banners, distance our ranks, and assault the enemy with a force equal to theirs.

10

Retreat as soon as we have engaged; beat the gongs to signal halting without actually stopping; continue for another three lis before turning back to counter-attack, at which time our ambush forces shall take advantage of the opportunity to rise and either attack the enemy's sides or strike their front and rear.

11

As long as the whole army fights valiantly, the enemy will be defeated and flee."

12

King Wu said: "Excellent!"

# GONGS AND DRUMS

1

King Wu asked Taigong: "When our army is deep into the territory of an enemy state and the enemy and us are equal in strength; the weather is freezing or scorching, or it rains heavily day and night for more than ten days; the ditches and fortresses are all destroyed; the mountainous passes cannot be guarded; the scouts are slack; and the soldiers are negligent, what should we do then if the attackers come at night and our three armies are unprepared and the general and soldiers are confused?"

2

Taigong replied: "All armies are strengthened if they are on guard, but if they are lax they will fail. Tell our troops to keep up sending and answering orders in the camp; sentries shall hold flags and communicate with each other inside and outside the camp, passing orders to each other; do not let the sound of gongs and drums be cut off; soldiers shall face the enemy and be ready to engage in battle.

3

Every three thousand men shall be formed into a cantonment, and be strictly admonished and restrained, so that they will each be careful to keep guard.

4

Then if the enemy come to attack, they will be deterred by our highly-disciplined soldiers. At that time, when the enemy are exhausted, we shall send our elite troops to attack immediately."

5

King Wu asked: "If the enemy know that we will chase them, and they mobilise their elite troops for ambush and then pretend to retreat; and if our army enters the enemy's ambush area and the enemy turn around to attacks us; some attack our front troops, some attack our rear troops and some charge into our camp, causing panic and disrupting our formations, what should we do in such a situation?"

6

Taigong replied: "We should divide our army into three squads and follow the enemy in separate groups, taking care not to enter the enemy's ambush area, and make sure all three units can catch up with the enemy at the same time before entering the enemy's ambush area. Then send some troops to attack the front and rear of the enemy and some to attack their sides; and give strict orders to the soldiers to move forward quickly. In this way the enemy will be defeated."

## SEVERED ROUTES

1

King Wu asked Taigong, "When our troops are deep into the enemy's territory and are confronting them, at this time, the enemy have cut off the food route of our army and have come around to the rear of our army, attacking us from both the front and rear. It does not bode well and we cannot stay on the defensive for long. What should we do?"

2

Taigong replied: "Whenever we are fighting in enemy territory, you must understand the geographical situation and take advantage of the terrain, relying on mountains, forests, rivers and trees to strengthen our position. Guard the passes and bridges carefully and tightly, and also master favourable terrain such as cities and mounds and graveyards. In this way, our defence will be solid, and the enemy will neither be able to cut off our army from the roads nor be able to detour to our rear and attack our army from both sides."

3

King Wu asked: "When our army is passing through tall mountains, wide swamps and flat terrain, the troops that have promised to meet us do not come on time and we suddenly encounter the enemy army. What should be done in such a situation?"

4

Ta Kung replied: "The general method of unifying an army for battle should be to first send out a reconnaissance team to the far side, and when we are two hundred lis from the enemy, we shall know the accurate location of the enemy.

5

If the terrain is unfavourable to our movements, we shall advance forward in battalions with martial chariots and send two rearguard units to follow behind, with the rearguard and the main forces spaced at a distance of one hundred lis from each other or fifty lis from each other.

6

In the event of an emergency, they can rescue each other from front to back. If our army can maintain this perfect and solid deployment, it will certainly not suffer casualties and defeats."

7

King Wu said: "Excellent!"

# OCCUPYING ENEMY TERRITORY

1

King Wu asked Taigong: "When our troops have taken advantage of the victory to charge into the enemy's state and capture their land, there is still a large city that we have not yet captured.

2

Meanwhile, there is another enemy force outside the city that is holding on to the dangerous terrain and confronting our army.

3

If we want to besiege the city but are afraid that the enemy troops outside the city will attack and join forces with the enemy inside the city to assault us on both sides, which will cause chaos and fear among our troops, what should we do in such a situation?"

4

Taigong replied: "Whenever we are attacking a city, we shall deploy chariots and cavalry at a distance from the city to act as guards so as to cut off the enemy's contact between inside and outside of the city.

5

In so doing, the enemy inside the city will inevitably be cut off from food for a long time because supplies from outside cannot be imported.

6

In this way, there will be panic among the enemy soldiers and people within the city, and the enemy general defending the city will inevitably surrender."

7

King Wu asked: "When the enemy inside the city are deprived of food and food cannot be imported from outside, they are secretly in contact with each other inside and outside of the city, plotting to break out our siege and fight to the death in the darkness of the night. Some of the enemy's elite chariots and horsemen are attacking me inside and some outside, causing fear and confusion among our soldiers and it seems that a defeat is imminent. What should be done in this situation?"

8

Taigong replied: "In such a case, we should divide our army into three parts and station them carefully according to the terrain.

9

Find out where the enemy's troops are located outside the city and the condition of the nearby large fortresses, and then leave a path for the besieged enemy to lure them out of the city. However, we must stay alert so as not to let them escape.

10

As the besieged enemy are panic-stricken, they will either try to escape into the mountains or retreat to another city or town.

11

At this point, we shall use one part of our army to first drive away the enemy's troops outside the city, and another part of our elite chariots and horses at a distance from the city to stop the escaping enemy from breaking out our defence outside the city.

12

In such a situation, the enemy forces inside the city will mistakenly believe that their fleeing troops have successfully broken out and opened a retreat route for them, and their elite soldiers inside the city will definitely continue to flee, leaving only old and weak soldiers inside. Then, with our third unit of chariots and cavalry, we shall drive deep and long into the enemy's rear.

13

In this way, the enemy defenders will not dare to continue their breakthrough.

14

At this point, we shall be extremely cautious and not rush into battle with the enemy, but simply cut off their food routes and surround them.

15

When we have captured a city or town, do not burn the grain in its storehouses; do not destroy the houses of its people; do not cut down the trees of its cemeteries or the jungles of its temples; do not kill the soldiers of the enemy who have surrendered; and do not mistreat the captives.

16

This is to show mercy to the enemy's people and display magnanimity.

17

Then announce to the enemy's soldiers and people: 'The only one who is guilty is your despicable ruler.' In this way, the world will be pleased and convinced."

18

King Wu said: "Excellent!"

## INCENDIARY WARFARE

1

King Wu asked Taigong: "When our troops are deep into the enemy's territory, we encounter dense grass and trees surrounding the army. At this time, the enemy take advantage of the dry weather and the swift wind to set fire to our troops upwind, and make their chariots and horsemen ambush the rear of our army, causing my three armies to panic, scatter and flee. What should we do?"

2

Taigong replied: "In this case, we shall erect ladders and flying towers at camps, and ascend to the heights to look out and carefully observe the situation in front and behind.

3

When we find the enemy burning a great fire, we shall immediately set fire on the open ground furtherer in front of our army to extend the area burned by the fire, and at the same time set fire behind our army in order to burn a black ground.

4

If the enemy come to attack, we shall withdraw to this black ground where the grass and trees have been burned.

5

The enemy who come to attack will see the fire in the open ground and surely retreat.

6

Our army will then take up positions on the black ground, covering our left and right flanks with strong crossbows and continuing to set fire to the grass in front and behind us.

7

In this way, the enemy will not be able to harm me."

8

King Wu asked: "What should we do if the enemy set fire both to our left and right, and to our front and rear, so that the smoke covers our army, and the enemy army suddenly attack the black ground we are holding?"

9

Taigong replied: "In such a case, we shall form our army into a combat formation and cover the left and right flanks with strong crossbows. This approach will not lead to victory, but it will not lead to defeat either."

# EMPTY FORTIFICATIONS

1

King Wu asked Taigong: "How can we know the weaknesses and strength of the enemy's camp and the movements of the enemy's troops to and fro?"

2

Taigong replied: "A general must know the adversities of heaven and the seasons, the dangers and convenience of terrain, and the gains and losses of men.

3

Climb to the top and look down in order to observe the changes in the enemy's situation; look at the enemy's camp from a distance to know their weaknesses and strength; observe the movement of the enemy's soldiers to know their organisation."

4

King Wu asked: "By what means can we truly understand them?"

5

Taigong replied: "If we do not hear the drums or bells of the enemy camp; and if we see many flying birds that are not frightened above the enemy camp and no dust in the air, we can tell that it must be an empty camp, and that the enemy are only using some dummies to deceive us. The fact that the enemy have not retreated far and have not stopped and returned in haste is a sign that they have moved too hastily. If they hurry in their movement, there will be disorder in front of and behind their troops. Without order, their ranks are bound to be in chaos. In such a case, we shall rush out to strike, and even if we are to strike a large number with a small number, we would surely be victorious."

CHAPTER V.

# LEOPARD SECRET TEACHINGS

# FOREST WARFARE

1

King Wu asked Taigong: "When our army is deep into the enemy's territory, we march in a forest and confront the enemy and we both occupy a corner of the forest. What should we do if we want the defence to be secure and the attack to be victorious?"

2

Taigong replied: "Deploy our army in a rushing formation in places where it is easy to fight with bows in the outer unit of the formation and halberds and shields in the inner unit of the formation; cut down grass and trees and open wide the roads so that our army can move in battle.

3

This is what is known as forest warfare.

4

In forest warfare, banners are hung high and the whole army is strictly restrained so that the enemy do not know about our situation.

5

The method of fighting in the forest is to mix our soldiers who use different weapons such as spears and shields into battle groups.

6

When the forest is sparsely wooded, we shall use cavalry to assist us and place chariots in front, and fight when we find an advantage and stop when we do not.

7

In the forest, there is a lot of dangerous terrain, so we must deploy in a rushing formation to prevent the enemy from attacking the front and rear of our army.

8

Therefore, the forces must be able to fight quickly and courageously.

9

In this way, even if the enemy outnumber us, they will be defeated and flee.

10

During the course of the battle, our troops must take turns to fight and rest, and all units move in formation.

11

This is the general principle of fighting in forest."

## EXPLOSIVE WARFARE

1

King Wu asked Taigong: "The enemy are driving straight into our territory, plundering our land, cattle and horses. The enemy army are swarming and approaching our city; our soldiers are in great fear and the people are being held captive. Under these circumstances, what should we do if we want to be able to defend and win?"

2

Taigong replied: "An enemy army like this is called an explosive enemy.

3

The enemy's cattle and horses must be short of fodder, and their soldiers must be without food, so they attack fiercely.

4

In such a case, we shall order our troops stationed far away to select the best soldiers and quickly attack the enemy's rear, calculating the timing of the attack so that those soldiers will meet our troops in the city at nightfall and the whole army will join together to fight the enemy quickly and fiercely.

5

In this way, though the enemy is numerous in number, the enemy general can be captured by us."

6

King Wu asked: "If the enemy army is divided into three or four units, they attack us with one unit in order to encroach on our land, and station with one unit in order to plunder our cattle and horses. When their main forces have not yet arrived, they already send one unit of soldiers to advance towards our city, causing panic in our army. What should we do in this situation?"

7

Taigong replied, "We should observe the situation carefully, and before the enemy have fully arrived, we should perfect our defence and stand by. Build an encampment four *li* from the city; spread out the gongs, drums and flags, and send another force as an ambush.

8

The troops in the camp are to concentrate their powerful crossbows and set up a concealed gate at every one hundred steps for attack, with barriers such as horses in front of the gate, chariots and cavalry outside the camp, and brave warriors in ambush.

9

When the enemy arrive, we shall first send our light-armed troops to engage the enemy; then pretend that we are defeated and retreat, and have our defenders set up banners and drums on the city wall to prepare for a full defence.

10

The enemy will think that our main forces are defending the city and therefore are bound to charge into the city.

11

At this point, we shall suddenly send out ambush troops to break into the enemy's formations or attack from outside.

12

At the same time, we shall order our whole army to attack quickly and fight bravely, charging both the front and the rear of the enemy.

13

Then even their brave warriors cannot hold on and their light-armed ones cannot escape. This method of warfare is called explosive warfare.

14

Even though the enemy are numerous in number, their general will surely be defeated and flee."

15

King Wu said: "Excellent!"

## STRONG ENEMY

1

King Wu asked Taigong: "When our troops are deep into the enemy's territory and come into frontal contact with the enemy's assault force, the enemy outnumber and outmatch us and are using the cover of darkness to attack either on our left flank or right flank, causing our whole army to be terrified. What should we do if we want to be able to win on the offensive and be firm in defence?"

2

Taigong replied: "Such an enemy is called an enemy of shock. To fight against them, our army is better suited for attack than for defence. We shall select strong crossbows and use chariots and cavalry as the left and right flanks, and attack the enemy's front with swiftness, and the enemy's flanks and rear with speed. We shall also attack both the outside and inside of the enemy formation. In this way, the enemy soldiers will be in confusion, and their general will be terrified and defeated."

3

King Wu asked: "If the enemy intercept our front from afar; attack our rear with haste; cut off our elite troops; block our reinforcements, and cause our front and rear to lose contact, then our whole army is disrupted and scattered and flees; our soldiers have no fighting spirit, and the general has no intention to hold the ground. What should we do in this situation?"

4

Taigong replied, "Your Majesty are asking a profound question! In such a case, one shall clearly examine the call to arms and send out the brave and elite soldiers; each one shall hold a torch and two men beat the same drum; find out the exact location of the enemy and then launch an attack either on the outside of the enemy or on the inside of the enemy. During the attack, our troops shall wear coded signals so that they can identify each other while extinguishing the torches and stopping drum-beating. After this they shall respond to each other both from inside and outside, and all the troops move according to the pre-agreed plan. When the whole army strikes swiftly and fiercely, the enemy will surely fail and perish."

5

King Wu said: "Excellent!"

## MARTIAL ENEMY

1

King Wu asked Taigong: "When our troops are deep into the enemy's territory and, we are suddenly confronted by a large and fierce enemy, who surrounds our left and right flanks by large chariots and brave cavalry; our whole army is terrified and flee and cannot be stopped. What should we do about this?"

2

Taigong replied: "Such an army is called a defeated army. Those who are good at using their armies can win; those who are not good at using their armies can thus be defeated."

3

King Wu asked: "What should be done to deal with such a situation?"

4

Taigong replied: "We should equip our ambush troops with strong crossbows, and deploy powerful chariots and valiant cavalry on the left and right flanks. The ambush soldiers are usually placed about three lis in front and behind our main forces. If the enemy come to chase us, our chariots and cavalry shall be deployed to attack the enemy's left and right flanks, so that the enemy army will be caught in confusion while our fleeing soldiers will stop trying to escape."

5

King Wu asked: "When the chariots and cavalry of the enemy and our troops meet, the enemy are many while we are fewer, and the enemy is strong while we are weak. The enemy come to attack with a neat formation and sharp weapons. What should we do if we want to fight against them but find it difficult to withstand them?"

6

Taigong replied: "In this case, we shall select the strongest soldiers and crossbows and ambush the enemy on the left and right, and set up the chariots and cavalry in a strong formation for defence. When the enemy pass through the place where we plan ambush, we shall relentlessly shoot at their left and right flanks with powerful crossbows, and send out our chariots and cavalry and warriors to attack them violently, either at their front or at their flanks and rear. In this way, the enemy, though numerous in number, will surely be defeated by us."

7

King Wu said: "Excellent!"

# CROW AND CLOUD FORMATION IN THE MOUNTAINS

1

King Wu asked Taigong: "When our troops are deep into the territory of an enemy state, we encounter a high mountain and a huge rock with high peaks and no grass or trees, and are surrounded by enemy troops. Our whole army is in fear and our soldiers are confused and in disarray. What should we do if we want to be able to defend, strike back and win?"

2

Taigong replied: "Whenever an army is deployed on top of a mountain, it is easily isolated by the enemy; whenever an army is deployed at the foot of a mountain, it is easily besieged and trapped by the enemy. When fighting in a mountainous region, we must set up a crow and cloud formation.

3

That is to say, we must be on guard for all directions of the mountain. Our army shall either be stationed on the north side of the mountain or on the south side of the mountain.

4

If we are stationed on the south side of the mountain, we shall guard the north side of the mountain; if we are stationed on the north side of the mountain, we shall guard the south side of the mountain; if we are stationed on the left side of the mountain, we shall guard the right side of the mountain; if we are stationed on the right side of the mountain, we shall guard the left side of the mountain.

5

Every place on the mountain where the enemy can climb is to be guarded, and the main roads and passable valleys are to be blocked with chariots.

6

The banners shall be hoisted high for communication, and the three armies shall be kept in strict formations so that the enemy will not be aware of our agenda, thus forming a mountain defence.

7

The ranks of our troops shall be arranged; the soldiers shall be mobilised; the decrees shall be issued; the use of the regular and ad-hoc tactics shall be determined, and the troops shall be formed into a rushing formation and placed on the peaks of the hills where they can easily fight.

8

Then the chariots and cavalry shall be deployed in a formation of a crow and cloud. In this way, when the enemy strike, our whole army will fight back fiercely. Then the enemy army, though numerous in number, will be defeated and their general captured by us."

# CROW AND CLOUD FORMATION IN THE MARSHES

1

King Wu asked Taigong: "When our troops are deep into the enemy's territory and confront them across the river, the enemy have plenty of resources and a large army, while our army is poor in resources and weak in strength.

2

We want to cross the river to attack, but cannot afford to advance; we want to delay the advance, but we lack food.

3

Moreover, our army is in a barren land, with no cities or grasses nearby, and there is nowhere for our army to acquire resources and for our cattle and horses to graze. What should we do?"

4

Taigong replied: "When our army has no war preparations, the cattle and horses have no fodder, and our soldiers have no food; we shall look for opportunities to deceive the enemy and move quickly elsewhere, and set up ambush troops behind them to block the enemy's chase."

5

King Wu asked: "If the enemy is not deceived by us; if our soldiers are confused and fearful; if the enemy disrupt our army in front and behind, and if our whole army is routed, what should be done?"

6

Taigong replied: "The main way to seek a retreat at this point is to lure the enemy to come with gold, silver, and treasures; at the same time, bribe the enemy's emissaries. This must be done with precision and care without the enemy finding out our plan."

7

King Wu asked: "If the enemy have detected that we arrange an ambush, instead of crossing the river, they have sent a small army to attack us, causing panic in our troops. What should be done?"

8

Taigong replied: "In this case, we shall deploy our army in a fourfold formation and station where it is easy to fight.

9

After the enemy army has all crossed the river, we shall send our ambush troops to attack the enemy's flanks and rear violently with strong crossbows shooting at the enemy's left and right sides.

10

At the same time, our chariots and cavalry shall be arranged in a formation of crow and cloud, alerting the front and rear, so that the whole army can assault fiercely.

11

When the enemy discover that our army is engaged with their small forces, their large army will surely come across the river. At this point, we shall send our ambush soldiers again to attack the enemy's rear and use our chariots and cavalry to attack the enemy's two flanks, so that despite their large size, the enemy will be defeated and their general will surely flee.

12

The basic principle of the use of troops is that when facing the enemy, our army shall be arranged in a rushing formation in a place where it is easy to fight. And then the chariots and cavalry shall be deployed in a formation of crow and cloud, which is the way to win by ad-hoc tactics. The crow and cloud formation resembles flying birds and clusters of clouds; it is flexible and infinitely changeable."

13

King Wu said: "Excellent!"

## THE FEW AND THE MANY

1

King Wu asked Taigong: "What should we do if we want to strike the many with the few and the strong with the weak?"

2

Taigong replied: "To strike the many with the few, we shall use the time of dusk to deploy ambush soldiers in deep grassy terrain and intercept the enemy on a dangerous and narrow road. To strike the strong with the weak, we shall seek assistance of a large state and the support of neighbouring states."

3

King Wu asked: "If we have no deep grassy areas to set up ambush and no dangerous roads to use; and the enemy's army arrives at a time other than dusk; and we have neither the assistance of a large state nor the support of our neighbours, what should be done?"

4

Taigong replied: "We shall use bluffing and deception to confuse the enemy's general, and lure them into a detour advance, so that they must pass through the deep grassy land; we shall delay their marching, so that they will engage us just at the time of dusk. When the enemy's leading troops have not all crossed the water, and their succeeding troops do not have time to camp, we shall launch ambush troops to attack the enemy's two flanks quickly and violently, and send chariots and cavalry to disrupt the enemy's front and rear. In this way, the enemy, though numerous in number, will be defeated. Respectfully serve the king of a large state; courteously treat the wise men of our neighbouring states; send generous gifts to them; and speak humbly so that we will be able to gain the support of a large state and the assistance of neighbouring states."

5

King Wu said: "Excellent!"

# DIVIDED VALLEYS

1

King Wu asked Taigong: "When our troops are deep into the enemy's territory, we confront them in a dangerous and narrow place. Our army is on the left side of the mountain and the right side of the water, while the enemy's army is on the right side of the mountain and the left side of the water. In this situation, each side wants to defend to be secure and attack to be victorious. What should we do?"

2

Taigong replied: "When our army occupies the left side of the mountain, we shall quickly guard the right side of the mountain; when we occupy the right side of the mountain, we shall quickly guard the left side of the mountain.

3

If there are no boats available to cross rivers in the dangerous areas, use floating equipment to cross.

4

The leading troops who have already crossed the rivers shall quickly open up the way forward and seize favourable terrain so that the main forces can follow.

5

The front and rear of our troops shall be covered by chariots, and strong crossbows shall be deployed so that our ranks and formations are stable.

6

For the main roads of communication and valley crossings, the chariots shall charge forward to block the routes.

7

Flags and banners shall be hoisted, thus forming a defence connected by chariots.

8

The method of fighting in the most dangerous areas is to place the chariots in front, protected by large shields with strong crossbows to safeguard our left and right flanks.

9

Every three thousand men shall be formed into an offensive unit and deployed on terrain that is easy to fight.

10

Our left army is used for the left flank, the right army for the right flank and the central army for the central place in formation, with the three armies attacking side by side while advancing.

11

The troops that have fought return to their original camps to rest, and those that have not fought are put into assault, fighting and resting in turn until victory is achieved."

King Wu said: "Brillant!"

CHAPTER VI.

# CANINE SECRET TEACHINGS

# DISPERSING AND ASSEMBLING

1

King Wu asked Taigong: "What should the king do when he leads his troops on an expedition and the three armies station in several different places while the general wants to assemble the army to engage the enemy on schedule, to send orders to officers and soldiers, and to specify a system of reward and punishment?"

2

Taigong replied: "When it comes to managing military, due to the large number of the three armies, there are bound to be changes in the deployment of dispersing and assembling formations. The supreme general shall first determine the location and date of the battle, and then issue the battle documents to the commanders of all the troops, specifying the cities to be attacked and besieged, the places where each army will assemble, and the date of the battle and the time of arrival of each unit.

3

The general then arrives early to set up his camp and formations, and erects a pole at the camp gate to observe the sun's shadow and calculate the time.

4

Ordinary people are forbidden to pass and soldiers and commanders report for duty. When the commanders arrive, the order of their arrival is verified. Those who arrive first shall be rewarded, while those who arrive late shall be beheaded.

5

In so doing, they will arrive at the meeting camp on schedule regardless of distance.

6

When all three armies have arrived, they will be able to concentrate their efforts on engaging the enemy."

# MILITARY VANGUARD

1

King Wu asked Taigong: "The important principle of using the army is that there must be powerful chariots, valiant cavalry and vanguard troops capable of charging into battle and launching an attack when they see an opportunity for the enemy to take advantage of it. What exactly is the right moment to launch an attack?"

2

Taigong replied: "To attack the enemy, one shall perceive in detail the fourteen circumstances that are unfavourable to the enemy. Once these situations arise, an attack can be launched and the enemy will certainly be defeated."

3

King Wu asked: "Would you elaborate on these fourteen circumstances that are unfavourable to the enemy?"

4

Taigong replied: "An attack can be launched when the enemy have just assembled and are not yet firmly established; an attack can be launched when the enemy's men and horses have not eaten and are hungry; an attack can be launched when the weather and seasons are unfavourable to the enemy; an attack can be launched when the terrain is unfavourable to the enemy; an attack can be launched when the enemy is rushing; an attack can be launched when the enemy is not on guard; an attack can be launched when the enemy is tired and weary; an attack can be launched when their general has left his men without command; an attack can be launched when they have travelled a long distance; an attack can be launched when they have crossed a river; an attack can be launched when they are hurried and disorganised; an attack can be launched when they have passed through a dangerous and narrow road; an attack can be launched when their ranks are scattered and disorganised; an attack can be launched when and they are in fear and anxiety."

## SELECTING WARRIORS

1

King Wu asked Taigong: "What should be the method of selecting warriors and forming military units?"

2

Taigong replied: "Those in the army who are superb in courage and are not afraid of death and injury shall be formed into a group called the heroic squad; those who are vigorous, young and brave, strong and fierce shall be formed into a group called the storming squad; those who are remarkable in physique and skilled at using long swords, and walk steadily and move neatly shall be formed into a group called the sharp squad; those whose arms are so strong that they can straighten iron hooks, and who are so strong and powerful that they can disrupt the enemy's formations and smash their gongs and drums and tear their banners shall be formed into a group called the valour squad; those who were once noble ministers who have lost their power and wish to rebuild their success shall be formed into a group called the duel squad; those who are the sons of fallen generals and are eager to avenge their fathers and brothers shall be formed into a group called the death squad; those who used to marry into their wives' family and are captives who want to redeem themselves shall be formed into a group called the aspiration squad; those who are poor, angry and disaffected and want to be rewarded for their contribution shall be formed into a group called the determination squad; those who have been exonerated and want to cover up their shame shall be formed into a group called the pardon squad; those who are talented and can take daunting tasks shall be formed into a group called the standby squad. This is the method of selecting warriors and forming units for the army, which must not be left unexamined."

## TEACHING COMBAT

1

King Wu asked Taigong: "What should be the training method to assemble the whole army and to train the soldiers to be skilled in combat?"

2

Taigong replied: "Whenever one is in command of the three armies, he shall use gongs and drums to command.

3

This is to make the whole army move neatly and uniformly.

4

The general must first tell the officers and soldiers clearly how they should be drilled, and must affirm and explain clearly over and over again, and then train them in the handling of weapons, in familiarising themselves with battle movements according to the changes in the command signals of the various flags.

5

Therefore, when training an army, one must first train a single soldier, and when the training of a single soldier is completed, ten men will train together; when ten men learn the methods of warfare, the training is completed, and then a hundred men will train together; when a hundred men learn the methods of warfare, the training is completed, and then a thousand men will train together; when a thousand men learn the methods of warfare, the training is completed, and then ten thousand men will train together; when ten thousand men learn the methods of warfare, the training is completed, and then the whole army will train together; when the whole army learns the methods of warfare, the training is completed, and then a million men will train together.

6

In so doing, a mighty army can be established, and its might is invincible.

7

King Wu said: "Excellent!"

# EQUIVALENT FORCES

1

King Wu asked Taigong: "How many infantrymen can one chariot withstand? And how many infantrymen can stand up to one chariot? How many cavalrymen can withstand one infantryman? And how many cavalrymen can one infantryman challenge? How many cavalrymen can one chariot withstand? And how many cavalrymen can confront a chariot?"

2

Taigong replied: "Warriors are the wings of an army; they have great fighting power and are used to attack and trap the enemy, intercept the strongest enemy and break their retreat; cavalry are the eyes of an army and can be used to scout and warn, follow and pursue the fleeing enemy, cut off the enemy's food routes and attack the scattered and roaming enemy.

3

If chariots and cavalry are used inappropriately, a cavalryman will be no match for an infantryman.

4

If the whole army is arranged in formation and the chariots, cavalry and infantry are properly coordinated, then the rule of thumb for fighting on flat terrain is that one chariot can hold off eighty infantrymen, and eighty infantrymen can hold off one chariot.

5

One cavalryman can hold off eight infantrymen, and eight infantrymen can hold off one cavalryman.

6

One chariot can hold off ten cavalrymen, and ten cavalrymen can hold off one chariot.

7

The rule for fighting on dangerous terrain is that one chariot can hold off forty infantrymen, and forty infantrymen can hold off one chariot.

8

One cavalryman can hold off four infantrymen, and four infantrymen can hold off one cavalryman.

9

A chariot can hold off six cavalrymen, and six cavalrymen can hold off one chariot.

10

Chariots and cavalry are the most powerful fighting force in the army; ten chariots can defeat a thousand of the enemy, and a hundred chariots can defeat ten thousand of the enemy.

11

Ten cavalrymen can defeat a hundred of the enemy, and a hundred cavalrymen can defeat a thousand of the enemy.

12

These, of course, are approximate estimates."

13

King Wu asked: "What should be the allocation of the number of officers in charge of chariots and cavalry and what is their combat method?"

14

Taigong replied: "The number of officers that a chariot should have is: five chariots for a chief, ten chariots for a commander, fifty chariots for a officer, and a hundred chariots for a general.

15

The method of fighting on flat terrain is to have five chariots in a line with each line forty steps apart from the front and rear lines and ten steps apart from the left and right lines; each squad of chariots is sixty steps apart from the front and rear squads and from the left and right squads.

16

The method of fighting on dangerous terrain is that the chariots must advance along the road, with ten chariots in a cluster and twenty chariots in a unit.

17

The distance between chariots is twenty steps apart from the front and rear chariots and six steps apart from the left and right chariots. The distance between squads of chariots is thirty-six steps apart from the front and rear squads as well as from the left and right squads.

18

Five chariots are managed by a chief with a range of operation of two *li*; as the chariots withdraw from the battle, they return by the same way they leave.

19

The number of officers to be provided for the cavalry is one commander for five cavalrymen, one official for ten cavalrymen, one leader for a hundred cavalrymen and one general for two hundred cavalrymen.

20

The method of fighting on flat terrain is to have five cavalrymen in a line with each line twenty steps apart from the front and rear lines, and each cavalryman four steps apart from the left and right men; the distance between each squad of cavalrymen is fifty steps apart from the front and rear squads as well as from the left and right squads.

21

The method of fighting on dangerous terrain is: each line of cavalrymen is ten steps apart from the front and rear lines and two steps apart from the left and right lines; each squad of cavalrymen is twenty-five steps apart from each other in all four directions.

22

Thirty cavalrymen are formed into a unit and sixty cavalrymen a section with an officer for every ten cavalrymen, whose range of operation is one hundred steps.

23

They shall return to their original positions after withdrawing from battle."

24

King Wu said: "Excellent!"

# MARTIAL CHARIOT WARRIORS

1

King Wu asked Taigong: "What is the method of selecting martial warriors for the chariots?"

2

Taigong replied: "The criteria for selecting chariot warriors are: they are under forty years old and over seven *chi* five *cun* tall; they are as fast as a galloping horse; they can jump onto a chariot in the midst of a run; they can fight on all sides of a chariot; they can command flags and banners; they can use a full eight-stone crossbow and shoot arrows skilfully. Such men are called martial chariot warriors, and they must not be treated without any preferential policies."

## MARTIAL CAVALRY WARRIORS

1

King Wu asked Taigong: "What is the method of selecting martial cavalry warriors?"

2

Taigong replied: "The criteria for selecting cavalry warriors are: they are under forty years old; they are over seven *chi* five *cun* tall; they are strong and agile and able to move more quickly than ordinary men; they can ride a horse at a gallop and shoot arrows with a bow on it; they can fight on all sides of a horse and advance and retreat with skill; they can ride a horse over ditches and valleys, climb hills, rush over dangers, cross waters and chase and disrupt strong enemy. Such men are called martial cavalry warriors, and they must not be treated without any preferential policies."

## CHARIOTS IN BATTLE

1

King Wu asked Taigong: "What is the method of warfare for chariots?"

2

Taigong replied: "Infantry warfare is about being familiar with changes in the situation; chariot warfare is about being familiar with the terrain, and cavalry warfare is about being familiar with other short cuts. Chariots, infantry and cavalry are all combat units, but they are used differently. There are ten deadly situations and eight favourable ones in chariot warfare."

3

King Wu asked: "Which are the ten deadly situations?"

4

Taigong replied: "A chariot that can advance but cannot retreat is a situation of death.

5

A chariot that overcomes a dangerous obstacle and chases the enemy over a long distance is a situation of exhaustion.

6

A chariot that faces flat terrain in front but difficult terrain behind is a situation of distress.

7

A chariot that is trapped in a dangerous obstacle and difficult to get out is a situation of extinction.

8

A chariot that is destroyed in a muddy area with water is a situation of labour.

9

A chariot that has a dangerous obstacle on the left and a flat surface on the right while climbing up a slope is a situation of disadvantage.

10

A chariot that rides on grassy land and has to cross deep water is a situation of frustration.

11

Chariots that are insufficient on flat terrain and do not work well together with infantry is a situation of defeat.

12

A chariot that faces ditches behind, deep water on the left and high slopes on the right is a situation of doom.

13

A chariot that cannot move forward or backward when it rains heavily day and night for days and the roads are destroyed is a situation of dilemma.

14

These ten types of situations are all deadly for chariots.

15

So an incompetent general is bound to be defeated and captured because he does not understand the dangers of these situations, whereas a wise general is victorious because he can avoid these situations."

16

King Wu asked: "Which are the eight favourable situations?"

17

Taigong replied: "When the enemy's front and rear lines are not yet set, use the chariots to attack.

18

When the enemy's flags are in disorder and men are constantly moving, use the chariots to attack.

19

When some of the enemy's soldiers are moving forward and some are moving back, some to the left and some to the right, use the chariots to attack.

20

When the enemy's formation is unstable and the soldiers are hesitant, use the chariots to attack.

21

When the enemy is advancing with indecision and retreat in fear, use the chariots to attack.

22

When the enemy is congregating in disarray, use the chariots to attack.

23

When the enemy is fighting on flat terrain but show no signs of victory, use the chariots to attack.

24

When the enemy has travelled far but the battle is still not over by sunset, and the whole enemy troops are in fear, use the chariots to attack.

25

These eight situations are all favourable to chariot warfare.

26

If the general knows the above ten deadly situations and eight favourable situations for chariot warfare, he can win every battle even when his army is surrounded by the enemy who attack his troops with thousands of horses from the front and both sides."

27

King Wu said: "Brillant!"

# CAVALRY IN BATTLE

1

King Wu asked the Taigong: "What should be the method of battle for cavalry?"

2

Taigong replied: "There are ten victories and nine defeats in cavalry combat."

3

King Wu asked: "Which are the ten victories?"

4

Taigong replied: "When the enemy have just arrived and their formations are not yet stable, and there is no connection between their front and back forces, we shall immediately assault the enemy's leading cavalry unit with our cavalry and disrupt their two flanks, then the enemy will surely flee; when the enemy's formations are neat and strong and their soldiers are highly motivated, our cavalry shall keep assaulting the enemy's two flanks and not let go by running back and forth as fast as wind and as fierce as thunder and keep fighting from daylight to dusk and changing flags and costumes constantly, then the enemy will be frightened and confused and we shall be able to defeat them; when the enemy's formations are not strong and the soldiers have no fighting spirit, then we shall use our cavalry to advance on the enemy's front and rear, attack their left and right and disrupt their two flanks, then the enemy will be terrified.

5

When the enemy have no dangerous terrain to hold on to, we shall drive deep and cut off the enemy's food route, then the enemy will surely be starved; when the enemy are on flat terrain and are vulnerable to attack on all sides, we shall attack with cavalry and chariots, and the enemy will surely be routed; when the enemy are defeated and their soldiers are scattered, we shall attack from both flanks or from the front and rear, and then the enemy's general will be captured; when the enemy return to their camp at dusk, and their troops are numerous but in disorder, we shall deploy cavalry to form a unit of ten, a squad of a hundred, a group of five chariots and a section of ten chariots with many banners and strong crossbows to either disrupt their flanks or cut off their front and rear, so that the enemy's general will be captured. These are the ten opportunities for victory in cavalry combat."

6

King Wu asked: "Which are the nine defeats?"

7

Taigong replied: “Whenever we attack the enemy with cavalry and fail to break through the enemy’s formation, and the enemy pretend to flee but attack our rear with chariots and cavalry, this is the defeat of breakdown.

8

When we chase fleeing enemy, cross dangerous terrain, and drive long and deep without stopping, and the enemy deploy ambush to our left and right and cut off our rear, this is the defeat of besiege. When we cannot retreat after advancing and cannot enter and are caught in dilemma, this is the defeat of death.

9

When the road ahead is narrow and the road behind is winding, and the enemy can attack the strong with the weak and the many with the few, this is the defeat of collapse.

10

When deep valleys and woods make movement difficult, this is the defeat of exhaustion.

11

When there are rivers on the left and right, and mountains in front and behind, and our army is fighting the enemy between two rivers and the enemy occupy key locations in mountains and rivers, this is the defeat of hardship.

12

When the enemy have cut off our rear food route, and our army can only advance and has no way to retreat, this is the defeat of obstruction.

13

When there are muddy roads and swamps that make it difficult to advance and retreat, this is the defeat of impasse.

14

When there are deep ditches on the left and pits on the right, and roads seem to be flat but are actually uneven, and both advance and retreat will attract enemy attacks, this is the defeat of entrapping. There are the nine defeats for cavalry in battle.

15

These are the situations that a wise general tries to avoid, and an incompetent general fails to avoid."

## INFANTRY IN BATTLE

1

King Wu asked Taigong: "What is the method of fighting infantry against chariots and cavalry?"

2

Taigong replied: "When fighting infantry against chariots and cavalry, we shall arrange formations according to hilly areas and dangerous terrain by placing long weapons and strong bows in the front and short weapons and weak crossbows in the back, and taking turns to fight and resting more often. When the enemy's chariots and cavalry arrive in large numbers, we shall hold our formations and fight stubbornly, and keep the soldiers and strong crossbows on guard to the rear."

3

King Wu asked: "If there are neither hills nor dangerous terrain to rely on and the enemy are arriving in large and powerful number; if their chariots and cavalry assault our two flanks as well as our front and rear, causing our whole army to fear and flee in disarray, what should we do?"

4

Taigong replied: "Order our soldiers to make obstacle devices such as caltrops and chevaux de frise, and group the cattle and horses together and form the infantry into a fourfold rushing formation.

5

When they see the enemy's chariots and cavalry approaching, they shall place caltrops widely and dig circular trenches, each of which is five chis wide and deep and called a 'life cage'.

6

Our infantry shall move in and out with their horses, and form a camp squad with chariots connected to it, pushing it backwards and forwards; and when it comes to a halt it becomes a temporary camp.

7

Guard the right and left sides with strong crossbows and warriors, and then call upon our whole army to fight fiercely and relentlessly."

8

King Wu said: "Excellent!"